America's Highest Destiny

The Causes of Nine-Eleven and a Bold Vision of America's Role in the World

Roger L. Plunk

1st WORLD LIBRARY
The World's Publisher

Austin, Texas

**America's Highest Destiny
the Causes of Nine-Eleven and a Bold Vision of
America's Role in the World**

Roger L. Plunk

© Roger L. Plunk, 2003
1st World Library
8015 Shoal Creek Blvd., Ste. 100
Austin, TX 78757
www.1stworldlibrary.com

First Edition

Senior Editor
Rodney Charles

Cover Design and Production
Amelia Nottingham-Martin

Library of Congress Card Catalog Number: 2002095399

ISBN: 1-887472-01-0

To Mom and Dad,
Lillian Jean Meabe Plunk, ever-unfolding flower of love,
& Lt. Col. William Gerald Plunk, U.S. Air Force (Ret.),
Cold War fighter pilot,
who embody America's two powers in foreign relations:
Compassion and Defense.

And so today, in this year of war, …we have learned lessons…

We have learned that we cannot live alone, at peace; that our own well-being is dependent on the well-being of other nations far away. We have learned that we must live as men, not as ostriches…

We have learned to be citizens of the world, members of the human community.

We have learned the simple truth, as Emerson said, that "The only way to have a friend is to be one."

So we pray to Him now for the vision to see our way clearly – to see the way that leads to a better life for ourselves and for all our fellow men – to the achievement of His will to peace on earth.

- President Franklin D. Roosevelt
Fourth inaugural address, 1945

CONTENTS

Preface   iii

Part One: Afghanistan

Breakfast With Massoud   3
Portrait of a Failed Policy   9
The Taliban, Al-Qaeda, and Pakistan   14
The Northern Alliance   22
Kashmir   28

Part Two: Israel and Palestine

Seeds of Conflict   37
Security Council Resolution 242   44
The Peace Process   49
Nine-Eleven Politics   53
Bush's Challenge   60

Part Three: Iraq

Iraq's Stalin   73
Gulf Wars   80
Betrayal   89
War by Sanctions   94

Part Four: Highest Destiny

Formula for Peace   105
America, Democracy, and Human Rights   111
America's Lost Vision   120
A Bold New Policy   124

PREFACE

When the proverbial butterfly flutters the air on one side of the world, it is said to influence events on the other side. The fluttering butterfly is a common illustration of the interconnectedness of the world we live in. A butterfly's influence is too small to be of much concern. But when American foreign policy-makers flutter their wings, tidal waves of change can crash on the far shores of the world, and then echo back to the shores of America. Those changes are either for the better or for the worse.

The attack on America on September 11, 2001 was the result of failed American policy echoing back to American shores. America failed in Afghanistan because it did not counter the rise of the Taliban and al-Qaeda. America failed in Israel because it did not force a just peace settlement between Israel and the Palestinians. And America failed in Iraq because it did not promote democratic reforms or remove Saddam Hussein from power.

The result of this failed policy has been despair, frustration, and anger, the fuel of terrorism. From these failures, rivers of anger flowed forth, merged into an ugly alchemy, and attacked America. Clearly, the individuals ultimately responsible for Nine-Eleven are those who hijacked the airliners and flew them into the World Trade Center and the Pentagon. But we cannot ignore the underlying causes.

Nine-Eleven awakened America to the consequences of its actions, and to its responsibilities in the world. As the world's only *superpower*, America has a higher responsibility than other countries. It must lead the world in fighting tyranny in its many forms. It must be the impartial world sheriff.

But America also has the responsibility to lead the world in promoting democracy, human rights, and peace. This is *moralpolitiks*, the use of wealth and knowledge to build a better world. This is America's heart and soul. This is America's best and highest destiny.

In Part 1, *Afghanistan*, I write from my own experiences, having been a non-government mediator there in 1998. In Part 2, *Israel and Palestine*, and Part 3, *Iraq*, I write as a political analyst sitting on the sidelines. In these three parts of the book I review America's policy mistakes. Essentially, these mistakes resulted from ignoring the central role of *moralpolitiks*. In Part 4, *Highest Destiny*, I attempt to formulate a new policy, based on the promotion of democracy and human rights.

In writing this small book, my purpose was to present a clear overview, unadorned with scholarly fluff. I tried to avoid getting lost in the great complexity and convoluted histories of these conflicts. I tried to focus only on those basic forces at play that seem relevant for understanding these conflicts and the impact of American policy. And I tried to keep it short.

Part One: Afghanistan

BREAKFAST WITH MASSOUD

In April of 1998, I had breakfast with "commander" Ahmad Shah Massoud at his home in Panjshir Valley, Afghanistan. I had just spent two months in Panjshir as a non-government mediator. I was there getting his input for a policy on national reconciliation that I was mediating among the leaders of Afghanistan's Northern Alliance. That was done. Now he wanted to talk to me about the future of Afghanistan and American policy.

Massoud's official title was "defense minister," but he was the *de-facto* leader of the alliance. He was a great hero in the Afghan war against the Soviets. For this reason, and because the Afghan war was instrumental to the fall of the Soviet Union, *The Wall Street Journal* once called him "The Afghan who won the Cold War." But for the Afghans, he was known as the "Lion of Panjshir." Panjshir means five lions, so it translates as the "lion of five lions." There is an old Afghan saying that anyone who wants to conquer Afghanistan should beware, because under every rock of every mountain lies a sleeping lion. When Massoud was fighting the Soviets, they said, "And the lion is Ahmad Shah Massoud!"

At this time (1998), Massoud held the front line north of Kabul against the Taliban, who viewed him as their last great obstacle for conquest of Afghanistan. A few months before I arrived in Afghanistan, the Taliban had taken considerable amounts of territory. Mullah Omar, the Taliban leader, offered Massoud a sweet deal (money and an official position with the Taliban). Massoud called his war council together, placed his round wool hat on a table, pointed to it and declared, "As long as I have this much territory, I will fight." The Taliban were pushed back soon afterwards.

I was saddened when I heard that suicide bombers assassinated Massoud on September 9th 2001, just two days before the attack on America. His assassins have been connected to bin Laden. This makes sense. Massoud was bin Laden's greatest enemy inside Afghanistan. This was made clear to me that morning at breakfast.

In Afghanistan, meals are traditionally eaten on the floor, sitting cross-legged around a cloth that serves as a dining table. Massoud himself spread the cloth out and served the food. Spring air flowed into the room, and the morning sunlight splashed around us. Peering out the window, I saw almond trees in full bloom and heard birds chirping. After the meal, Massoud sat back and made a long presentation on his policy. I wrote it down in my notebook, occasionally asking for clarification.

Massoud shared his vision of a peaceful Afghanistan. It was a vision of democracy, human rights, and a federal system where power would be shared between the national government and local governments. The obstacles to peace were the Taliban – who wanted to force all Afghanistan under its oppressive policies – and Pakistan and the foreign terrorists who supported the Taliban. Massoud explained that America had initially supported the Taliban. He was not convinced that this had changed, and wanted to develop good relations with America.

Massoud asked me if I thought bin Laden was a threat to America. I told him, "Bin Laden has the desire and the resources to buy a nuclear weapon and float it up the Potomac River to Washington DC." He nodded in agreement. With the backing of America, he assured me, the Northern Alliance could rid Afghanistan of all terrorists.

My last memory of Massoud is of him sitting cross-legged on the floor by himself, looking down in deep thought and fingering a blade of grass. He was frustrated: Why wouldn't America support his efforts to topple the Taliban and destroy bin Laden's al-Qaeda terrorist network?

In August of 1998, al-Qaeda organized the bombing of American embassies in Kenya and Tanzania, killing about three hundred people and injuring about five thousand. The day after this tragedy, I contacted the head of the State Department's Afghan Desk, and conveyed Massoud's message: With American help he could rid Afghanistan of the Taliban and al-Qaeda. The State Department official rejected the idea with contempt.

Instead, the Clinton administration attacked some terrorist camps inside Afghanistan with cruise missiles. The missiles killed a few people, but had no influence on al-Qaeda. (They also attacked a pharmaceutical factory in Sudan, later found to be uninvolved with any terrorist activity.)

After the George W. Bush administration assumed office, I sent a long letter to Deputy Secretary Richard Armitage, hoping that a new administration would be open to a new policy. I again conveyed Massoud's message, but it was again rejected.

It was not that I was uniquely insightful of the threat of al-Qaeda. Bin Laden had declared war on all Americans (civilians and military) in 1998. Thus, America was already at war with al-Qaeda. All it takes is one party to declare war for war to exist. Bin Laden's declaration was given deeper significance when the media began reporting (in the same year) that he was trying to buy nuclear weapons.

Al-Qaeda's threat was also made clear by the bombing of the World Trade Center in 1993, by the bombing of American embassies in Africa in 1998, and by the bombing of the *USS Cole* in 2000. Al-Qaeda claimed responsibility for bombings that targeted American troops in Yemen in 1992, and for the downing of US helicopters in Somalia in 1993 (portrayed in the movie, *Blackhawk Down*). Al-Qaeda was also linked with a failed attempt to attack American and Israeli tourists in Jordan during the millennial celebrations, and failed plans to assassinate the Pope and President Clinton. All of this was public knowledge.

Many have argued that Nine-Eleven was an "intelligence" failure: The CIA and FBI should have been a little more aggressive, a little more cooperative in sharing information. But that argument misses the larger point. The threat was well known, and the only way to remove the threat was to remove al-Qaeda. There was no way for the CIA or FBI to defend America against every single terrorist attack. Even in 2002, after al-Qaeda had been decimated and at its weakest, American policy makers were still claiming that another attack was not only possible, but "inevitable." Nine-Eleven was not an intelligence failure. It was a policy failure.

By 1998 America had ample justification for supporting the Northern Alliance in its fight against the Taliban and al-Qaeda. The Northern Alliance was the military arm of the Republic of Afghanistan, still recognized by the United Nations. The Taliban was an excessively repressive regime destroying the peace of Afghanistan. And the Taliban gave refuge to terrorists responsible for hundreds of deaths, many of them American. Article 51 of the United Nations Charter provides the right of "individual and collective self-defense" to member states, which could have been interpreted as allowing America to come to the aid of Afghanistan's recognized government. And of course, America had the right of self-defense to intervene and protect Americans from future terrorist attacks.

All the justification under international law for intervention that existed after Nine-Eleven, existed years before

Nine-Eleven. American policy makers knew of the threat of al-Qaeda, and they had justification to act. What was lacking was willpower and inspired leadership.

Perhaps the greatest responsibility falls on the Clinton administration. They were on watch when al-Qaeda emerged as a clear threat. But the Bush Administration is not innocent. They should have adopted an aggressive policy early on. When the Bush administration entered office, America's greatest national security threat was al-Qaeda. An action-plan, developed by the interagency Counter Terrorism Security Group, was presented to the new Bush team in January of 2001. The plan called for supporting the Northern Alliance in order to collapse the Taliban and defeat al-Quaeda. Essentially, it called for the same policies America adopted after Nine-Eleven.

However, Condoleezza Rice, Bush's national security adviser, was more vocal about sinking the Kyoto treaty on global warming (which has nothing to do with national security). And for pushing for the proposed missile defense program, citing North Korea as a threat (N. Korea may be "pesky," but did not represent a real threat). Some commentators argued at that time that it was not nuclear weapons on missiles that America should worry about, but nuclear weapons coming to America by private plane, ship, truck, or the back of a donkey. Not a whimper was heard from the Bush administration about al-Qaeda.

PORTRAIT OF A FAILED POLICY

Afghanistan is the "crossroads of Asia." For ages, merchants and armies passed through Afghanistan, creating a colorful but often violent history. Alexander the Great, Genghis Khan, the British, and the Soviets all left their mark. Then the Americans came, first to counter the Soviets, then to make war on the Taliban and al-Qaeda. They are distinguished from earlier invaders by coming as liberators, not conquerors. True, they have not been the best of liberators. But despite this, Afghans, unlike some other Muslim cultures, have always liked Americans.

During the Cold War, America and the Soviet Union competed for influence in Afghanistan through aid programs. For example, whereas Soviets built roads running south to north (towards their borders), Americans built roads running east to west (towards Iran, then an ally). I have met a number of Afghans who remembered the "golden" years, when Afghanistan was full of American engineers, teachers, and agriculturists.

Soviet influence led to the rise of a communist government, whose policies soon became resented by the Afghans. When the government was on the verge of collapse in 1979, the Soviets invaded Afghanistan to prop it up, thus beginning ten years of *jihad* (holy war) between the *mujahadeen* (holy warriors) and the Soviets.

To counter the Soviet occupation of Afghanistan, America poured three billion dollars into arms for Afghans to fight the Soviets. This money was channeled through Pakistan. America gave Pakistan a free hand in choosing who would get this aid. This was the crucial decision that would have such vast consequences. It was the beginning of a failed policy.

Being at the crossroads of Asia, the Afghan culture is diverse. There are four major ethnic groups that correspond ethnically to the areas around Afghanistan. The largest group is the Pashtoons. They make up about forty percent of the population, and correspond to Pakistan. The Tajiks, comprising about twenty-five percent of the population, correspond to Tajikstan. The Uzbeks, comprising about six percent of the population, correspond to Uzbekistan. And the Hazara, a Shia minority, comprising about twenty percent of the population, correspond to Iran, a Shia Muslim country (the other groups are Sunni Muslim). I use the word "correspond" because there has been a lot of ethnic blending over the centuries. One can see traces of the Mongols in the Hazara and Uzbeks, and traces of Greeks in the Tajiks. And whatever their ethnic identity, they all consider themselves to be Afghans.

Pakistan chose to give the military aid to militant fundamentalists, primarily ethnic Pashtoons, and foreign Arabs like bin Laden. Massoud would have been a prime candidate for aid because he was Afghanistan's best field commander. But he got none of this aid because he was a "moderate," and a Tajik.

The reason why Pakistan gave all its support to Pashtoons, was that Pashtoons are also found in large numbers in Pakistan. The theory was that a Pashtoon dominated government in Afghanistan would support Pakistan's policies because of their ethnic ties to Pakistan.

Historically, a Pashtoon aristocracy ruled Afghanistan by dominating the other ethnic groups. Pakistan wanted to continue this arrangement. It was a failed policy, of course, because Pashtoon rule was feudal and oppressive, and the other groups would not willingly submit to it. They wanted to be part of the government, not oppressed by it.

When the Soviets withdrew in 1989, they left one million Afghan dead, five million Afghan refugees, and millions of land mines strewn throughout the land that continue to injure Afghans every day. A Soviet supported government struggled until it was finally overthrown by the mujahadeen in 1992. A new government was established, and civil war soon erupted. Rivalries between the mujahadeen were partly responsible. But those differences could have been resolved.

The main cause was Pakistan's involvement in Afghan politics. This dragged the country down into a whirlpool of civil war, causing tens of thousands of more deaths and plunging the country into severe poverty. Pakistan first put its support behind the Pashtoon commander Hekmyatar, who shelled Kabul for years, leaving it in rubble. Pakistan eventually withdrew its support from Hekmyatar, and put it behind the Taliban.

American policy makers considered Pakistan a "friend" in its fight against the Soviets. This relationship continued even after the Cold War ended. During the Clinton administration, Secretary of State Madeline Albright was asked why Pakistan was not on the annual list of countries that support terrorism. She answered that it was because Pakistan was our "friend." It was a policy of appeasement.

Thus as a "friend," America looked the other way as Pakistan gave American aid to militant fundamentalists, creating a war machine that eventually turned against the world. And America looked the other way as Pakistan promoted an oppressive Pashtoon government, turning Afghanistan into a war zone, and a sanctuary for al-Qaeda. The result was thousands of deaths, and unimaginable suffering from severe poverty, sickness, refugee problems, and lawlessness.

America should have directed its aid to moderates like Massoud during the Soviet occupation, and helped the Afghans build a democracy after the Soviets withdrew. American policy failed because it ignored the basics.

America bowed to the selfish policies of Pakistan, and ignored its higher moral responsibility to promote peace, minority rights, and democracy.

The Afghans felt betrayed. After the Afghans helped America defeat the Soviet Union, America left the fate of a weak and destroyed Afghanistan to the selfish interests of Pakistan. To his credit, President Bush, not long after Nine-Eleven, declared that America will not betray Afghanistan again. I hope America keeps that promise.

THE TALIBAN, AL-QAEDA, AND PAKISTAN

The popular story is that the Taliban arose in Kandahar as a movement to restore order in an Afghan countryside, ruled by warlords and former mujahadeen brigands. They were seen as heroes, protecting the weak against thugs with guns. Even the government in Kabul welcomed them, until they started shelling Kabul and demanding the government's removal. It is not clear whether the story of the Taliban as a homegrown movement is true or not. But whatever their origin, they soon got support from Pakistan. And with their help, the Taliban took Kabul in 1996, beginning a new era of civil war in Afghanistan. 1996 also marked the year in which Pakistan made arrangements for bin Laden to return to Afghanistan.

When I was in Afghanistan, I had a series of meetings with Taliban officials. The first thing I learned from my meetings was that they rejected any idea of reconciliation with the Northern Alliance. They had a policy of conquest and assimilation. They were open to allowing members of the opposition "join" the Taliban, but the Taliban leadership would remain intact. As I told one American diplomat, the Taliban were like *Star Trek's* "Borg," a race that assimilates all other races into its "collective." Haji Qadir, a Pashtoon leader in the Northern Alliance and close adviser to Massoud, once told me that "The peace of the Taliban is the peace of the graveyard." Qadir later became a vice president in the new transitional government, but was assassinated in July of 2002.

Despite the policy they embraced, the Taliban leaders I met never came across to me as evil. In fact, they were very friendly and sincere. They wanted to bring peace to Afghanistan and believed that they were the only ones who could do this. Many of them expressed deep sympathy for the Afghans suffering from poverty and violence due to the civil war.

One of these, Mullah Hassan, the governor of Kandahar, told me that he wanted to bring women back into the workforce and girls back into schools. I reminded him that Islam endorses the use of assemblies to resolve disputes, and suggested that a large assembly be formed to resolve the differences between the Taliban and the Northern Alliance. He smiled, and said, "Yes, yes, we can do that if the *Ulema* (religious leaders) agree." But of course they never agreed.

Such moderate views were opposed by the more numerous radical members of the Taliban, who composed their army and religious police; and by members of al-Qaeda, who were becoming very influential. Thus, the policy decisions of the Taliban always flowed along the radical vein: No work for women, no schools for girls, no reconciliation with the opposition.

"Taliban" is the plural form of the word "talib," meaning student, specifically religious student. There is a saying that if you want to start a revolution, go to the universities because students are full of energy, idealistic, and often gullible. That is what the Taliban did. Many of the Taliban were from the militant *madrassas* (Islamic schools) in Pakistan.

These madrassas were not the liberal colleges Americans are familiar with. They taught fundamentalism and militancy, far removed from true Islam. Muhammad taught religious tolerance and compassion, and was a reformer who gave women rights. These maddrasas preached prejudice, violence, and oppression. There are thousands of madrassas in Pakistan. Of these, a few hundred teach militant fundamentalism. And of these, dozens advocate the destruction of America.

The militant madrassas in Pakistan began during the Soviet occupation of Afghanistan when foreign Arabs came in great numbers to fight the "godless" Soviets. The ideology (Wahhabism) and funding of the madrassas came primarily from Saudi Arabia. Militant fundamentalism was thus a foreign ideology transplanted from the Middle East to Afghanistan and Pakistan. It was the bitter fruit of repressive governments like Egypt and Saudi Arabia. It preached the use of violence to overthrow secular governments in Muslim countries, and replace them with Islamic governments. And it thrived in the Afghan war against the Soviets, finding new resources and converts.

Because America supported Egypt, Saudi Arabia, and Israel (which many saw as oppressing the Palestinians), America was seen as the father of all enemies. Bin Laden, who was from Saudi Arabia, embraced this philosophy. When bin Laden was a child, his father told him that he should help to liberate Palestine from Israeli occupation.

Al-Qaeda, meaning "the base," was originally created by bin Laden as a base for Arab fundamentalists fighting against the Soviet "oppressors" of Islam in Afghanistan. It later evolved into a training base for terrorists. After training, these militants would go forth to promote their cause in the Middle East, Central Asia, South Asia, the Philippines, Russia (Chechnya), Europe, and of course, America. Their goal was to violently promote a pan-Islamic *"Emirate"* – an idealized form of Islamic government that would unite the Muslim world – and to expel non-Muslims from Muslim countries.

Militant fundamentalism united al-Qaeda and the Taliban. The Taliban leader, Mullah Omar, was declared to be the *Emir-ul-Momineen*, the leader of the faithful, implying that he was the supreme leader of the Muslim world. The Muslim world rejected this of course, or brushed it aside as a joke, but the Taliban took it seriously.

One of the easiest ways that America could have countered the rise of fundamentalism was to fund alternative education. Aid groups working in Pakistan noticed that when American funding for education was reduced in the 1990's, the number of madrassas increased. If young Afghans and Pakistanis had access to education that prepared them for jobs, these madrassas would not have had the students to teach hate and intolerance.

Alternative education would not have prevented militant fundamentalism, but it would have reversed its growth. And it would have transformed many lives. Young Afghans schooled in radical madrassas, who killed and died fighting in the battlefields of Afghanistan, might have had very different, peaceful lives.

Traditionally, the Afghan culture was tolerant of other religious traditions. This included other Muslim sects, as well as Hindus, Sikhs, and Jews. One indication of this tolerance was the popularity of Sufism, a non-dogmatic, Islamic mystical teaching. The rise of fundamentalism in Afghanistan reversed the Afghan custom of religious tolerance. When the Taliban were finally defeated, and the new interim government put in place, Afghan Sufis were seen dancing in the streets for joy.

During my stay in Afghanistan, I heard many stories from Afghans about Pakistani officers, including generals, working with Taliban military forces. I also met Pakistani prisoners being held by Massoud. And during my stays in Kabul, I heard a steady flow of large planes landing at the Kabul airport. These were Pakistani cargo planes bringing supplies. The Taliban did not have such planes.

I never knowingly met al-Qaeda members, but their presence became clear to me from my talks with Afghans, and by reports from journalists. The Taliban had evolved into a strange hybrid, composed of Afghan fundamentalists, Pakistanis, and al-Qaeda terrorists. It was a true axis of evil.

The Afghan fundamentalists made up the Taliban's formal leadership. Al-Qaeda's "Brigade 55" constituted the Taliban's strongest fighters, composed of about five thousand Arab soldiers. Al-Qaeda's leader, bin Laden, provided substantial amounts of funding, and became known as the Taliban's *de-facto* defense minister. Pakistan provided the Taliban with military and political support. Perhaps as many as ten thousand Pakistani soldiers fought with the Taliban. If you count advisers and logistical support, the number of Pakistanis involved in the Taliban war effort would be much greater. These three forces did not always get along, but they shared a common goal of defeating the Northern Alliance and establishing a Pashtoon dominated government.

After Nine-Eleven, President Bush demanded that the Taliban hand over bin-Laden. This was just a formality to show the world that the Taliban were given a chance to avoid war. But it was impossible for the Taliban to hand him over because he was part of their organization, and much too powerful. Thus, in order to destroy al-Qaeda, America had to destroy the Taliban. And to destroy the Taliban and al-Qaeda, America had to force the cooperation of Pakistan.

It took weeks of American pressure before Pakistan finally cut ties with the Taliban. But Pakistan had little choice. If they sided with the Taliban, the entire international community would have opposed them. Pakistan was like the owner of an attack-dog that had been faithful, but had bitten too many people. Pakistan had to put it to sleep, but was reluctant.

Pakistan's support of militant fundamentalism allowed a monster to grow. This militancy has become entrenched in the culture. Thus, when Pakistan cut its bonds with the Taliban and started cracking down on militant fundamentalism within its own borders, Pakistanis went into the streets to protest. And when the Taliban collapsed, and al-Qaeda was attacked, members of these groups sought refuge in Pakistan.

Pakistan's President Pervez Musharraf understands that militant fundamentalism could lead to Pakistan's "internal destruction." But he also fears that too much reform may lead to civil war. He has thus taken a cautious approach. Having taken years to evolve, militant fundamentalism will take years to be eradicated.

Perhaps his most important reform has been to outlaw the teaching of militancy in Islamic madrassas. He is turning off the faucet that pours out new militants. But he still has to deal with the militant culture that has grown up over the last couple of decades.

America, having failed to nip militancy in the bud, is now being forced to help Pakistan put a stake in the heart of a monster that refuses to die.

THE NORTHERN ALLIANCE

Before Nine-Eleven, the Northern Alliance was the only opposition to the Taliban and al-Qaeda in Afghanistan. Besides firing a few cruise missiles in 1998, America did nothing to counter the Taliban and al-Qaeda except for lobbying the United Nations to place economic sanctions on the Taliban. But this had little influence, except on the civilian population, who went from very poor to extremely poor. And because of the long and porous borders with Pakistan (who supported them), the Taliban still got much of what they needed. The Northern Alliance held the front line against al-Qaeda, America's greatest national security threat, while America frowned on giving them any support.

Because the Taliban were not interested in reconciliation, I spent most of my time with the Northern Alliance. The members of the Northern Alliance did not always get along. But they all realized that it was impossible for any one group to rule Afghanistan. They had to find a way to work together. Thus my time was spent negotiating a common policy of national reconciliation among them.

The Northern Alliance was composed of all the major Afghan ethnic groups: Pashtoon, Uzbek, Tajik, and Hazara. There were not that many Pashtoons because the territory the Northern Alliance controlled was non-Pashtoon. But I did meet some Pashtoon commanders and advisers. And of the nine members of the Northern Alliance that signed the agreement I negotiated, two were Pashtoon (one of these was the late Haji Qadir). This was significant because it demonstrated that the Northern Alliance was open to bringing Pashtoons into their organization.

The Northern Alliance was essentially an inclusive group. "Northern Alliance" was a name given by the media. Their chosen name was "United Front," which more accurately represented their policy of bringing all the diverse Afghan groups together.

Also important was that the Northern Alliance was willing to surrender power to neutral persons, that is, people who were not members of the Taliban or the Northern Alliance. This was a central point in the agreement I negotiated. The purpose of the agreement was to help demonstrate to the world that the Northern Alliance was committed to national reconciliation, not conquest. It was my hope that the agreement would help convince the international community, especially America, to get behind the Northern Alliance, develop them politically and militarily, and isolate the Taliban. This would force the Taliban to either reconcile with the Northern Alliance (I was always hopeful for a less violent solution) or collapse.

American diplomats rejected the idea of supporting the Northern Alliance because they claimed that leaders of the Northern Alliance were responsible for human rights abuses during the pre-Taliban civil war, and that Afghans did not have faith in them. This was an argument I heard Taliban leaders make on many occasions. It was an empty argument. Clearly, there was no reason to idealize the Northern Alliance. They had seen nothing but war for twenty-two years, and no doubt, atrocities were committed. But atrocities were not a matter of policy for the Northern Alliance.

When I visited Massoud's military headquarters in Panjshir Valley, I met prisoners of war and found them to be well treated. And at the request of (then) President Rabbani, I advised a woman official on how to form a human rights commission after the war was over. The important thing was that the leaders of the Northern Alliance were committed to building a democratic and human rights-based government for Afghanistan. They may not have understood democracy. But they knew it is what they wanted.

The Americans were saying that they did not want to work with the Northern Alliance because they had a tainted reputation. But if the Americans had worked with the Northern Alliance, they could have developed them politically, and improved their human rights practices, thus establishing faith among the Afghan people and the international community. That was the point. All the leaders of the

Northern Alliance I spoke to reached out their hands for this help but were rejected.

The main reason why America did not support the Northern Alliance was because of Pakistan's opposition. An American-supported Northern Alliance fighting a Pakistani-supported Taliban would be awkward for allies. Even after Nine-Eleven, Pakistan opposed the idea of American support for the Northern Alliance. It took weeks of American pressure for Pakistan to give in to the inevitable, and to withdraw their support (and troops) from the Taliban.

If America had put its support behind the Northern Alliance in 1998, after the bombings of the American embassies, more time could have been used to strengthen them. The Taliban would have been forced to collapse without the massive bombing campaign that delivered about twenty thousand bombs and killed as many as three thousand innocent civilians (despite efforts to avoid civilian casualties). Al-Qaeda would have lost its refuge, and Nine-Eleven might never have happened.

After Nine-Eleven, the Northern Alliance proved a faithful ally to America. It cooperated with American troops, and did most of the ground fighting against the Taliban and al-Qaeda. And it supported the international community in efforts to build a democratic and human rights-based government. True to their stated policy of surrendering power, President Rabbani (a Tajik) stepped down from power, and Hamid Karzai (a Pahstoon) was elected president. Others outside of the original Northern Alliance, including women, were also brought into the new government.

The history of Afghanistan is marked by the gradual concentration of power by the national government in Kabul. Before the Soviet invasion, all provincial government officials were appointed by the national government, leaving little or no local control. This created a single bottleneck through which all political power flowed, making it highly prone to power struggles. The Soviets and the Taliban took this to the extreme.

Thus members of the Northern Alliance have always been suspicious of any power in Kabul, fearing it may revert back to the old ways. They all prefer a unified Afghanistan, but one that will protect local power, and minorities such as the Hazara. As a way to accomplish this, Massoud once described to me his plan for a federal Afghanistan that would establish a balance of power between the national government and the local governments.

Today (2002) most of the countryside is still ruled by "warlords," and the transitional government of president Karzai controls just the area around Kabul and the flow of foreign aid. One reason for this is that the warlords simply do not want to relinquish power. But a more fundamental reason is that they are afraid to relinquish power until they know that their areas will not once again be oppressed by an overpowering national government.

A major challenge in the next couple of years will be to define a government that will protect local interests.

The old battle-scarred leaders of the Northern Alliance will continue to be involved in doing this. The Northern Alliance has become like an irritating piece of sand in an oyster, upon which a new pearl is being formed.

KASHMIR

When the British de-colonized India in 1947, British India was divided into Pakistan (which included Bangladesh at the time) and India. Pakistan became an Islamic state, established on the theory that Muslims could not get proper representation in India. India remained a secular state (ironically with more Muslims than Pakistan) on the theory that all ethnic and religious groups could be fully represented.

Kashmir was one of more than five hundred principalities that were not part of British India. They had their own king and administration, but were under the sovereign umbrella of the British. Thus, from a purely legal point of view, the principalities became independent when Britain withdrew. But that was just legal theory. As a political matter, independence was not an option for them. Many of these kingdoms were small and inside of British India.

Many were principalities only in name, being administered directly by the British. The few larger ones were simply forced to join either Pakistan or India.

But Kashmir was unique. Kashmir bordered both Pakistan and India, and had a long history as a nation. The twelfth century historical work *River of Kings* traces Kashmiri history back to legendary events said to have occurred five thousand years ago and chronicled in the great Indian epic, the *Mahabarata*. Kashmir also had a unique culture, called *Kashmiryat*, that transcended religious and ethnic ties. For these reasons, the *maharaja* (great king) of Kashmir refused to join either Pakistan or India, asserting his legal claim for independence.

Because the majority of people in Kashmir were Muslim, Pakistan insisted that it join Pakistan. India, embracing all faiths, felt that Kashmir should have an equal right to join India, but should not remain independent. Both countries treasured Kashmir because of the great beauty of its mountains, valleys, and lakes.

Pakistan tried to resolve the issue by force, and the maharaja of Kashmir appealed to India for protection. India agreed to help on the condition that Kashmir join India, subject to the consent of the Kashmiri people once order was established.

Kashmir signed a "treaty of accession," joining India, and India came to its aid. Although a cease-fire was arranged, order was never fully established. Kashmir became divided by what became known as the "Line of Control" between the Indian and Pakistani military forces. Through United Nations mediation, India and Pakistan agreed to have a plebiscite to determine the wishes of the Kashmiris. But the plebiscite never took place.

Two other wars were fought (in 1965 and 1971), and there have been decades of low-level conflict, placing the Kashmiri people in the crossfire between Indian troops and militant groups supported by Pakistan. In 1998, India and Pakistan came close to war sparked by the unexpected testing of nuclear bombs, first by India, then by Pakistan. In 1999, India and Pakistan clashed at a remote area in Kashmir called Kargil. It was the first time in history that two nuclear powers fought directly against each other. And in 2002, tensions rose so high that there was again fear of a nuclear war.

When I was in India in 1994, I drafted a peace initiative, and promoted it to the Kashmiris and the Indian government. The initiative advocated autonomy for Kashmir. (Autonomy places most power in the local government, allocating very limited powers, such as foreign affairs, to the national government.) The initiative also advocated accepting the Line of Control as the international boundary, and maintaining a "porous border" so that Kashmiris could easily go between Pakistani Kashmir and Indian Kashmir. This became a popular solution (not by my efforts) and was eventually embraced by the Indian government.

Under the Indian constitution, India has sovereignty over Kashmir only in the areas of military, international affairs, and communication. All other sovereign powers are reserved for Kashmir. But India began gobbling up Kashmir's autonomy in the 1980's, ruling it directly from Delhi.

Kashmiris resented the loss of autonomy, resulting in civil unrest. Pakistan used this as a rationale for supporting "freedom fighters." It was hoped that restoring autonomy for Indian Kashmir would remove Pakistan's rationale, and provide a basis for a political solution.

The Line of Control represents an equitable division between Pakistan and India. Pakistani Kashmir is composed of Muslims with close cultural ties to Pakistan. Indian Kashmir consists of Ladakh (originally part of Tibet) composed mostly of Buddhists; Jammu, composed mostly of Hindus; and the Vale of Kashmir, composed mainly of Muslims. The Vale of Kashmir is the historical Kashmir, and is the only real area of dispute between Pakistan and India. The Hindus and Buddhists in Indian Kashmir clearly prefer India. And the Muslims in Pakistani Kashmir clearly prefer Pakistan.

Kashmiris in the Vale of Kashmir have generally preferred independence, but would accept autonomy under a secular India that would respect their unique culture, *Kashmiryat*. Kashmiryat is a blend of religion, language, and traditions that forms something unique and distinct from other regions in South Asia. Like the Afghan culture, Kashmiryat is influenced by Sufi mysticism. But in addition to Sufism, Kashmiryat has also been influenced by the mysticism of Tibetan Buddhists and the Hindu yogis. Kashmiris are not simply Muslims or Hindus, but Kashmiri Muslims or Kashmiri Hindus.

1994 was a time of innocence for me. I did not realize until much later, that such a peace initiative was doomed because of the rise of foreign militants fighting in Kashmir. There was a possibility for reconciliation between India and the indigenous Kashmiris fighting for autonomy or independence; or even with those fighting to join Pakistan. But it was impossible for India to reconcile with the foreign militants. They were based in Pakistan, often trained in Afghanistan, and had no connection with the culture of the Valley of Kashmir. Two of the camps that were struck by American cruise missiles in Afghanistan in 1998 were being used to train militants to fight in Kashmir.

They were a foreign power. They began slowly coming into Kashmir in 1989, the year the Soviets began withdrawing from Afghanistan. Their purpose was to push out non-Muslims and force India to surrender the Valley of Kashmir to Pakistan. They made war against Sufis, and other moderate Muslims resisting their radical agenda, often by executing their leaders. It was a violent assault on Kashmiryat.

As militancy grew in Kashmir, so did the number of Indian troops to combat it. This has resulted in extensive human rights abuses by Indian troops. Understandably, the Kashmiris have come to resent both Pakistan and India. This has made independence much more attractive to them.

America's lack of resolve to stop the rise of militant fundamentalism in Pakistan resulted in a new cycle of violence in the Vale of Kashmir. Rooted in an ideology foreign to Kashmir, it devastated the culture, causing thousands of deaths and injured lives. And it brought two countries to the brink of nuclear war. When a superpower is negligent, whole cultures are destroyed.

In 2002, America pressured Pakistan to prevent militants based in Pakistan from fighting in Kashmir. This prevented a war. A decade of militancy will be difficult to reverse, but America's efforts have established the good faith necessary for peace to develop.

Establishing genuine autonomy in Kashmir (in both Pakistani and Indian Kashmir), and accepting the Line of Control as the international border is a sound political solution. But the people of Kashmir should be consulted. They were promised on two occasions to be consulted on the future of Kashmir: Once in the agreement between India and the maharaj of Kashmir, and once in the UN-negotiated agreement between India and Pakistan. These agreements should be respected.

Pakistan has always advocated a plebiscite to resolve the conflict, but has always limited it to two choices: Kashmir may join either Pakistan or India. They must consider expanding these choices. In resolving conflicts, it is crucial that solutions are not limited. There must be some flexibility for creative thinking. Dispute resolution is inherently a creative process.

There are many possibilities. The Vale of Kashmir could be made an autonomous region under the joint sovereignty of India and Pakistan. Or the Vale of Kashmir could be given its independence, with porous borders, making it a free trade zone between India and Pakistan. It would thus become a Zone of Peace between India and Pakistan, instead of a zone of war.

Once the larger issue of militant fundamentalism is overcome in Pakistan and Afghanistan, it is even possible for Afghanistan to become a Zone of Peace, a nation without a military, at the crossroads of Asia. This is one of the visions that Massoud was exploring, and which he touched upon at breakfast that fine spring day in 1998.

America, having failed so utterly in the past, now has the opportunity to lead Afghanistan, Pakistan, and Kashmir from endless conflict to lasting peace. It is a fitting mission for a great nation.

Part Two: Israel and Palestine

SEEDS OF CONFLICT

For centuries the Jewish people were dispersed throughout the world. They were the Jewish "Diaspora," a nation of people without a territory. Like Gypsies, they lived as minorities in other nations, often oppressed, yet amazingly capable of preserving their culture. In the mid 1800s, Jews being persecuted in Russia and Eastern Europe began migrating to Palestine, the Holy Land. It was the land of Jerusalem, their cultural center, their Mecca.

Zionism, an international Jewish movement, took up the challenge of establishing a homeland in Palestine. At that time, Palestine was a province of the Ottoman Empire, with a Muslim culture. The Ottoman government rejected the idea of any formal arrangement for a Jewish homeland, but allowed Jews to immigrate and establish settlements.

By 1880, the Jewish population had grown to about 24,000, out of a total population of about 700,000 people.

When the Ottoman Empire fell after World War I, the League of Nations gave Britain a "mandate" over Palestine. Under the mandate, Britain was to administer Palestine until it was able to administer itself, becoming independent. When the mandate began in 1922, Palestine consisted of what we know today as Israel, and the "occupied territories" claimed by the Palestinians. The mandate incorporated the British policy of supporting a "home" for the Jewish people in Palestine. The Jewish home was not envisioned as a state, but simply as a community within a state, that would not infringe upon the rights of the indigenous Palestinians, primarily Arabs, who lived there. Jews and Arabs were envisioned to live in harmony.

A Jewish home in Palestine made good sense, considering that Palestine was their cultural center, and that Jews being persecuted in Russia and Eastern Europe needed refuge. But problems soon emerged. The Jews that settled in Palestine brought European culture. And with large amounts of money, western education, and modern skills, they bought property and built closed communities. They soon became resented and viewed with suspicion as a colonial force with designs to take over Palestine.

Thus were the seeds of conflict planted: Persecuted Jews saw Palestine as their homeland, and a place of spiritual refuge. Arabs saw the immigrating Jews as a colonial power imposing a foreign culture.

The British did their best to reconcile the Jewish settlers with the indigenous Arab population. They offered the Jews and Arabs each the right to establish an "agency" so that they could work as partners with Britain in administering their local affairs. The Jews accepted, establishing the Jewish Agency. But the Arabs rejected the idea, fearing the rise of a Jewish state. It was a bad decision for the Arabs because they lost the opportunity to develop their own administration.

A massive flow of Jewish immigrants began in the 1930s due to Nazi persecution, and escalated due to the holocaust in World War II. The British advocated a single state of Palestine, where Jews and Arabs could share power. But Jewish settlers demanded their own state. And the Arabs protested against the immigration of so many European Jews and the emergence of a *de-facto* Jewish state. The British, unable to resolve the growing tension, and bleeding from a war with Jewish guerrillas fighting for a Jewish state, gave the issue over to the United Nations.

In 1947, the UN General Assembly passed a resolution announcing its solution to divide Palestine into a Jewish state and an Arab state. The two states would be united economically, and Jerusalem would be an international city.

America was the dominant force in the UN, and was instrumental in the decision to divide Palestine. President Harry Truman personally made efforts to convince UN delegates to favor this solution. The six million Jews recently killed in Nazi death camps, and the thousands of Jewish refugees seeking a home formed the compelling background for this decision. This resulted in over-whelming sympathy for the Jewish people and a sense of urgency to create a Jewish state.

General George Marshall, Secretary of State under Truman, and the "architect of victory" of World War II, understood the plight of the Jewish people. But he also understood that forcing a Jewish state would begin a war.

A big issue was the boundaries of the two states. Because Arab states rejected the idea of a Jewish state, they had refused to be part of the UN decision-making process. The result was that Arab interests were not protected. The boundaries decided for the Jewish state had more land in proportion to population, and had most of the prime coastal land. The Arabs got a bad deal.

Marshall argued that the wisest course was a UN "trusteeship" over all of Palestine until the issues surrounding statehood were settled. This would have allowed America to lead an ongoing negotiation process with the Arab states.

There was already a Jewish administration, and a state was inevitable. The real need was not in forcing the creation of a Jewish state, but in developing a working rela-tionship between the growing Jewish community and the Arabs. What was needed was reconciliation, not imposition.

However, emotion ruled over wisdom. President Truman decided against the idea of a trusteeship, and a Jewish state was forced into existence at great cost in human suffering. The modern state of Israel came into existence on May 14, 1948. America was the first to recognize Israel, just eleven minutes after Israel declared itself a state. Jews throughout the world were exultant. It was the first Jewish state in nearly two thousand years. But the Arabs were furious. In their minds, Israel was created by foreign colonization, at the expense of the indigenous Palestinian population, and under unfair conditions.

The next day, Arab states (Jordan, Syria, Iraq, Lebanon, and Egypt) attacked Israel. Israel had a modern army, and was able to defeat the Arabs by the early part of 1949. Israel took about half of the land that had been planned for the Arab state. This included West Jerusalem, meant to be an international city. Jordan occupied East Jerusalem and the West Bank, and Egypt occupied the Gaza strip. Palestine now became Israel (populated by Jews and a minority of Palestinians), and the occupied West Bank and Gaza (populated by stateless Palestinians).

––––––––––––––––––

During the 1948 war, Jewish radicals massacred most of the people in the Palestinian village of Deir Yasin, creating a wave of fear and a massive flow of hundreds of thousands of Palestinian Arabs from Israeli territory. These were the people who established the "refugee camps" (like Jenin) currently in the West Bank and Gaza strip. Because their absence created a large Jewish majority in Israel, they were not allowed to return to their homes in Israel, and lost their property left behind.

Israel's refusal to allow the Palestinians to return was, of course, a violation of international law that recognizes the "right of return." If I leave America because I am afraid of persecution or just don't like the place, I have the right as an American to return at any time. The American government can't keep me out just because they do not like me. Compensation for lost property and the "right of return" for these refugees continues to be fundamental issues for Palestinians. Lasting peace cannot be achieved without addressing these issues.

The Jewish people came to Palestine to escape persecution, bloodshed, and genocide. They came in search of a homeland, a place of refuge and peace. But at their moment of exultation in declaring their state, they suddenly found themselves surrounded by enemies, fighting for their lives.

The Palestinians sought to maintain their identity in the face of a growing Jewish homeland. But they got a bad deal for their Arab state, then lost half of it to Israel during the war. What Israel did not take, Jordan and Egypt occupied. On top of all this, many of the Palestinians ended up as refugees.

General Marshall's fear of war came to pass, but even he did not envision that by 2002, it would still be going on. There have been fifty-four years of war in various stages, meaning fifty-four years of anger. Those who lived during the 1948 War had children who have also had children. And those children are now at the age to have children of their own. This anger has almost become genetic. For the Jews, it has developed into a culture of anger against the Arabs. For the Arabs, it has developed into a culture of anger against Israel. This translates into fifty-four years of Arab anger against America, the supporter of Israel.

This anger against America is the oldest source of fuel, feeding the fires of terrorism that eventually resulted in Nine-Eleven. There are other issues: America's support of the repressive governments of Saudi Arabia and Egypt, American troops on Saudi soul, and American sanctions against Iraq. There is also the clash of the old world with the modern world, the frustrations of young men, and the individuals prone to violence. But Arab anger against American support of Israel forms the original source of anger, upon which all other anger coalesces, like streams joining a long river.

SECURITY COUNCIL RESOLUTION 242

After the 1948 War, Israel fought three more wars against its Arab neighbors in 1956, 1967, and 1973. In the Six Day War in June 1967 (against Egypt, Jordan, and Syria), Israel pushed Jordan and Egypt back, and occupied the West Bank (including East Jerusalem), and the Gaza Strip. (Israel also took Syria's Golan Heights and Egypt's Sinai Peninsula.)

After the war, the United Nations Security Council passed resolution 242, directing Israel to withdraw from "territories occupied in the recent conflict." The Security Council also affirmed the basic principle in international law that nations may not take territory by conquest. There is no longer a "right of conquest." This law, codified in the UN

Charter, is the same law invoked by the UN when it demanded Iraq's withdrawal from Kuwait.

The peculiar thing about Security Council Resolution 242 is that it did not address the territories Israel took by force in the 1948 War. If international law were strictly applied, then the territory taken in 1948 should also be surrendered. The implication is that the international community was willing to accept the expansion of Israel that occurred in 1948, but nothing beyond that. It was as if they were saying: 'Okay, we will overlook the territory you took in 1948, but there will be no more territory by conquest.' It was a compromise between the application of a fundamental law and political realities. The internationally recognized boundaries of Israel thus became the "pre-1967 boundaries."

The purpose of the Security Council is to maintain international peace and security. Unlike the UN General Assembly, the Security Council can pass resolutions that are "binding" on states, and can be upheld by the use of force. It was the Security Council that gave the formal authorization for the war against Iraq when it invaded Kuwait. And it was the Security Council that then directed Iraq to dismantle all weapons of mass destruction, and placed economic sanctions on Iraq to enforce this directive. Thus, Security Council Resolution 242 does not represent merely a request, but an order. It represents a binding international obligation placed on Israel.

Israel accepted Security Council Resolution 242. However, Israel argued that it also had a fundamental right of self-defense. Because Israel's territory is small and easily invaded, it needed to occupy these territories to provide a buffer between itself and hostile neighbors. This was a legitimate argument and generally accepted. Under this argument, Israel had a right to occupy these territories as long as there was a real threat of invasion, and as long as the occupation was necessary for its defense.

However, Israel soon began to abuse the argument of self-defense. East Jerusalem, which was part of the occupied territories, was immediately annexed by Israel. Obviously, annexation was not necessary for self-defense. Israel also began building Jewish "settlements" in the West Bank and Gaza Strip.

One could understand the building of temporary military bases for defense purposes. However, establishing civilian settlements in occupied territories did not help Israel defend itself. In fact, it made Israel's defense more difficult. The settlements provoked the Palestinians, resulting in guerrilla raids against the settlers. Israel's defense now had to include protecting the settlements in the West Bank and Gaza.

In recent years, there has been no real threat of invasion from Arab states. The only threat has been from Palestinians fighting against Israel's occupation of their land. Israel occupies the land to defend itself against terrorism. But it is because of the occupation that there is terrorism.

The real purpose of the settlements was to gobble up the West Bank and Gaza little by little. The idea was to transform the occupied territories into Israeli territories, and then force the international community to accept it over time. Israel wanted to establish a "fact" on the ground that could not be reversed.

Israel did not want to annex the West Bank and Gaza, as it did East Jerusalem. The reason is that annexation would make the Palestinian residents "citizens" of Israel, and the Jewish population would loose their large majority status. Thus the solution was to establish islands of Israeli sovereignty (Jewish settlements) in the West Bank and Gaza, and then control the rest of it as a "territory" of Israel, but not as an integral part of Israel. The Palestinians living there would thus remain stateless non-citizens, or perhaps "second-rate" citizens of Israel without voting rights. Of course, the Palestinians did not like the idea.

This policy found strong support among the those who saw the occupied territory as a part of the idealized state of Israel that once existed in Biblical times under Kings David and Solomon. This policy created a division in Israeli politics between the majority of Israelis who wanted to trade territory for peace (in accord with Security Council Resolution 242), and a powerful minority who wanted to keep the occupied territories in violation of international law and common fairness.

The international community objected to both the settlements and the annexation of East Jerusalem. But little was done to enforce these objections. America also objected, but did not craft a working policy to force the removal of the settlements, or to restore East Jerusalem to Arab territory.

The Palestinians, having got a bad deal by the United Nations in the original boundaries drawn for an Arab state, and having lost fifty percent of that territory in the 1948 War, began loosing the rest of their territory by annexation and the establishment of settlements. We can see why they became increasingly frustrated.

When America objected to the rise of terrorism in Afghanistan and Pakistan, but did little to counter this growing threat, the result was Nine-Eleven. Likewise, when America objected to the growth of settlements and the annexation of East Jerusalem, but did little to counter this growing problem, the result has been decades of anger, violence, and profound human suffering among Palestinians and Israelis.

THE PEACE PROCESS

After the Yom Kippur War in October of 1973 (where Israel fought Egypt and Syria), America's mediation efforts under the Ford and Carter administrations culminated in the Camp David Accords (1977). Camp David marked the beginning of the Middle East peace process.

Egypt wanted Israel to return the Sinai Peninsula, Egyptian territory taken in the 1967 War. Israel was willing to withdraw from some of the Sinai, but insisted that it had to keep much of it for defense purposes. From Egypt's point of view, the Sinai had been part of Egypt since the times of the Pharaohs, and they could not let go of any of it. Thus they came to an impasse.

The interest of Egypt was sovereignty over the Sinai. And the interest of Israel was defense. Thus, the solution arrived at in Camp David was very simple: Demilitarize the Sinai and return it to Egypt. Israel got its defense (a demilitarized Sinai), and Egypt got its sovereignty over Sinai. In addition, Egypt agreed to recognize Israel and to establish peaceful relations. And Israel agreed to allow for the development of a self-governing authority for the Palestinians in the West Bank and Gaza. Camp David was a masterpiece, and has become a model for creative mediation.

The Sinai was demilitarized and returned to Egypt. And Egypt recognized Israel and established peaceful relations. However, a self-governing authority for the Palestinians remained unfulfilled until the Oslo Accords in 1993.

Oslo had all the right ingredients for peace. Israel agreed to begin withdrawing from the West Bank and Gaza, and to replace the Israeli military administration with a Palestinian administration (called the Palestinian Authority). Israel also agreed to begin negotiations (after two years) on the final status of the West Bank and Gaza, and on the issues of Jewish settlements, East Jerusalem, and refugees. Israel even pledged to seek more international aid for the West Bank and Gaza. Although it was not explicitly proposed, Oslo implied the creation of a future Palestinian state.

Israel withdrew from the Gaza and most of the West Bank, a Palestinian Authority was established, and Yassir Arafat was elected president in 1996. But there was no progress on other issues. The peace process floundered.

The problem was that Israel remained divided. A small but powerful minority wanted the occupied territories to remain under Israeli control, and rejected the peace process. The Likud party, Israel's political Right led by Benjamin Netanyahu and Ariel Sharon, championed their cause by promoting more settlements and rejecting any concession on East Jerusalem.

Between 1993 and 2002, the Jewish settlements in the West Bank doubled, from 100,000 settlers to 200,000 settlers. The Israeli government promoted settlements by providing land in occupied territories at one tenth the cost of land in Israel, subsidized the construction of settlements (reducing the cost of housing by half, compared to housing in Israel), and gave an income tax reduction for settlers. Schools, public transportation, and community activities were heavily subsidized. In all, Israel spent about one billion dollars a year to sustain and defend the settlements.

In September 2000, negotiations were being held to decide how a Palestinian capital could be established in East Jerusalem. A central issue was the Temple Mount. The Temple Mount is the third holiest place for Muslims (known to them as *Haram al-Sharif*) because it is where Muhammad is believed to have ascended to heaven. The Jews also consider it holy because a part of the west wall of the Temple Mount is believed to be the last remains of the temples of Solomon and Herod the Great, where redemption is supposed to take place when the Messiah comes.

Ariel Sharon (then the opposition leader) made a trip to the Temple Mount, protected by one thousand security guards. The trip was a symbolic gesture to proclaim Israeli sovereignty over East Jerusalem (meaning: no Palestinian capital here!).

Palestinians were infuriated. Their dream that East Jerusalem (or at least some of it) would be the Palestinian capital was threatened. With Arafat's encouragement, they protested in the streets the next day, throwing stones. Israeli police, attempting to control the protests, shot and killed four Palestinians, and injured two hundred. The violence escalated, and a war began between civilian suicide bombers on the Palestinian side, and a modern military on the Israeli side. The light of hope for a Palestinian state was put out, and the peace process died.

NINE-ELEVEN POLITICS

After the Nine-Eleven attack on America, Ariel Sharon, Prime Minister of Israel, and Benjamin Netanyahu, a former prime minister, both declared that Yasser Arafat was "Israel's bin Laden." The Sharon administration was trying to marshal all the anger Americans felt towards bin Laden and direct it against Arafat and the Palestinians. They were also attempting to focus America's attention on terrorism as the one single issue in the Middle East. Israel, the message went, was an innocent victim of evil terrorists, just like America.

Terrorism can never be justified. The killing of innocent people is an evil in and of itself, regardless of its political purpose. But the issue of terrorism, committed by a small group of Palestinians, should not be used as a smoke screen to cover up the legitimate interests of the Palestinian people as a whole. Sharon and Netanyahu were taking advantage of the suffering of Americans to promote their agenda. It was dirty politics.

Americans never accepted the comparison between bin Laden and Arafat. But the American media and politicians did become focused on terrorism. Little attention was put on the history of the Palestinian struggle, and their legitimate rights under international law. The interests of the Palestinians were swept under the rug by the continual denouncing of terrorism. Rarely was it pointed out that suicide bombers would not exist if the interests of the Palestinians were addressed. Clear evidence for this can be found in the 1990s: Violence went down when Palestinians saw hope for a Palestinian state, and violence increased only when progress towards a Palestinian state was being frustrated.

The wise course for American politicians would have been to come down hard on terrorism, while pushing hard for a political solution that addressed the long-standing issues of the Palestinians. American support of a fair political solution would have taken the wind out of the sails of the terrorists. But no such wisdom emerged. Emotions ruled the day. Politicians jumped into the rushing flood of popular sentiment, and all that was heard was the resounding drumbeat of the war on terrorism.

The White House began the silly practice of using "homicide bombers" instead of "suicide bombers" in all of its policy statements, as if such a linguistic change would help matters (it just obscured the meaning). Congress passed a resolution declaring its "solidarity" with Israel, and equating Israel's war against suicide bombers with America's war on terrorism. And Tom DeLay, the House of

Representative's Majority Whip, argued that the West Bank should be part of Israel, because it was once part of the biblical Israel. On top of all this, President Bush called Sharon a "man of peace."

The Palestinians know better. Sharon has been fighting since the 1948 war, and is known as an independent, aggressive soldier, with a history of using excessive force. In 1982 Sharon was the defense minister who organized the attack of Beirut, Lebanon, in attempts to destroy the Palestinian Liberation Organization (PLO). The heavy destruction of Beirut, and the large numbers of civilian casualties, led President Ronald Reagan to call the attack "another holocaust." The violence would have been much greater without Reagan demanding restraint and withdrawal.

After the PLO left Beirut, Sharon ordered Israeli troops to surround the Palestinian refugee camps of Sabra and Shatila, thought to contain members of the PLO. This was done in violation of his agreement with the international community to withdraw. He then allowed Lebanese militia, allied with Israel, to enter the camps. They killed eight hundred innocent refugees. An Israeli judicial commission determined that Sharon was responsible for the massacre, forcing him to resign as defense minister.

Sharon, as prime minister, has been just as aggressive in his fight against terrorism. Sharon's government responded to suicide bombers by attacking the Palestinian Authority (beginning in April of 2002), killing and arresting as many "terrorists" as they could find. The Palestinian office in East Jerusalem was closed, offices in the Gaza Strip were destroyed, Arafat's office in the West Bank was attacked and put under siege, and most of the Palestinian areas were reoccupied. Palestinians saw the attack on the Palestinian Authority as an attack on their dream for a Palestinian state.

According to international human rights organizations, Israeli defense forces have intentionally targeted civilians (probably as an act of revenge for civilian deaths from suicide bombers). Israel has also used military force with a callous disregard to civilians. In July of 2002, an Israeli warplane (an American-made F-16) bombed a residential area. The target was one man, the leader of the military arm of the terrorist group, Hamas. In the attack, five homes were destroyed, and fourteen innocent people were killed, including nine sleeping children. About one hundred and fifty people were injured.

Sharon called this attack a "great success for Israel," and congratulated the Israeli Air Force. But the only result of these deaths was a new cycle of suicide bombings, causing more deaths.

The world denounced the act. The Bush White House also denounced it, calling it "heavy-handed," a weak term for killing sleeping children. But the Swedes were more precise, calling it "a crime against international law and morally unworthy of a democracy."

Sharon's policy has been to beat the Palestinians into submission. This has been done by military and economic means. From September 2000 to July 2002, military action has resulted in the deaths of about fifteen hundred Palestinians, perhaps as many as half of them civilian "non-combatants." And about four hundred million dollars of damage was done to the infrastructure of the Palestinian Authority.

Israel's borders were closed to thousands of Palestinians who worked in Israel, and travel restrictions were placed on movements between Palestinian populations, causing the economy to shut down. As of July of 2002, about fifty percent of the Palestinian population was unemployed, sixty percent lived below the poverty line of two dollars a day, thirty percent of the children suffered from malnutrition, and many children suffered from trauma due to the violence.

The result of Sharon's policy of oppression has been hopelessness and despair. But it is hopelessness and despair that feeds terrorism. It created a vicious cycle. The only way to get rid of terrorism is to remove the hopelessness. And the only way to remove hopelessness is to give Palestinians real hope for the Palestinian state they deserve.

The Bush administration's first reaction to Sharon's invasion of the Palestinian Authority was to demand that Israel withdraw. But eventually Bush supported Sharon's actions with the blanket statement that "Israel has the right to defend itself."

We can see why the Palestinians are uneasy about Sharon's war to defend Israel against terrorism. For them, it was not simply a war against terrorism, it was a war against a Palestinian state. Palestinians know that Sharon is one of the chief architects of the settlement program in the occupied

territories, and has recently said that even the smallest settlement is as much a part of Israel as Tel Aviv. And they also
know that he opposes giving up East Jerusalem.

In Sharon's vision of a Palestinian state, Israel main-
tains control of all security, and Palestinians have control of
things like health and education. Israeli settlements in occupied territories and East Jerusalem would become Israeli
territory, connected by Israeli-only roads and protected by
Israeli troops. Palestinians see Sharon's war against terrorism
as a way to force Palestinians to accept this arrangement. But
it is an arrangement unacceptable to any Palestinian.

Clearly, the only way for Israel to achieve peace is
to reconcile with the Palestinians and its Arab neighbors.
But Sharon has rejected this path, and has chosen a path of
oppression and continued conflict.

For Palestinians, Sharon is the butcher of Sabra and
Shatila. But for the Israelis, Arafat is the great terrorist.
Arafat has been the leader of the Palestinians for thirty-five
years. Most of these years he headed the Palestinian
Liberation Organization in its war against Israel, and thus
has a long history of violence.

However, it is often forgotten that Arafat, in 1988,
led the Palestinians to renounce terrorism and recognize the
right of Israel to exist. And in the Oslo agreement, Arafat
agreed to accept Israel on the basis of the pre-67 boundaries. Before that period, the common thinking among
Arabs was that Israel should exist only within the original

pre-1948 boundaries set by the UN. Thus Oslo was a major concession for them. Accepting the pre-67 borders meant that the Palestinians would accept just twenty-two percent of the original Palestinian mandate for their promised Arab state (Israel retaining seventy-eight percent).

In the recent war with Sharon, Arafat has done little to control Hamas and other groups that sponsor suicide bombers. As of July 2002, this war has caused about six hundred Israeli deaths, more than eighty percent of them innocent civilians. And Arafat has exercised poor leadership, provoking anger and violence instead of defusing it. If Arafat had adopted the philosophy of "peaceful resistance" used by Mahatma Gandhi, he would have been much more successful. He would have denied the political Right in Israel the use of the war on terrorism as an excuse for reversing the peace process and making war on the Palestinian Authority.

But even without the suicide bombers, and even without Arafat, the three big issues of settlements, East Jerusalem, and refugees would still remain. The more fundamental problem has been the rejection of these interests by the radical Right in Israeli politics. This rejection was clearly stated when Yitzhak Rabin, responsible for the Oslo accords, was assassinated in 1995 by a Jewish radical. And it has been restated by the policies of the Sharon government.

If both the Israelis and the Palestinians had a Mahatma Gandhi for leadership, there would be peace. An Arafat plus a Sharon equals war. Thus the need of a strong mediator to intervene; thus the need for American involvement.

BUSH'S CHALLENGE

America is Israel's friend. America defeated Nazi Germany, and helped Israel come into existence. The Jewish-American community, an important part of America, has been a source of financial and moral support to Israel for a century, decades before it was even a state. And America and Israel share the same ideals for democracy. But friendship should never be unconditional. America should be the impartial mediator. As the world leader, it has a higher duty to rise above petty alliances, and apply the same standards to all. It should be as tough on Israel as it is on the Palestinians. This is Bush's ongoing challenge.

When the George W. Bush administration assumed office in 2001, they announced a "hands-off" policy: Israel and the Palestinians would work things out on their own, with America on the sidelines. This policy was in contrast to the Clinton policy of aggressively working for a political solution.

This hands-off policy emerged during the ongoing political battles of the Republicans to win back the White House. It was a way to distinguish themselves from the Democrats. The trouble with this policy was that it was little more than political rhetoric. A hands-off policy is not a working policy for promoting peace. Its only result has been to help the political Right in Israel, who found it much easier to pursue their interests without the intruding Americans.

The history of the Middle East peace process is a history of hard work by American presidents, often pulling their hair out in frustration. Camp David was not just President Jimmy Carter, but the culmination of the hard work by both the Ford and Carter administrations. And Oslo was the culmination of the hard work of the Reagan, Bush, and Clinton administrations. An American hands-off attitude never accomplished anything during these decades other than the unraveling of peace.

When one party to a conflict is stronger than the other party, the stronger party will dictate the terms. A mediator in such a conflict must balance the scales to insure that the interests of both parties are met. Otherwise, the weak party will end up with unfair conditions, making them simmer with frustration and resentment, eventually erupting in future conflict. Israel is the stronger party in this conflict, and America, the mediator, must actively protect the legitimate interests of the Palestinians, the weaker party.

After Nine-Eleven, Bush suddenly became engaged in the Middle East. For the first time in history, America publicly recognized the Palestinian right to have a state. Secretary of State Colin Powell, understanding the need for America to be the impartial mediator, always emphasized Palestinian interests as well as Israeli interests. But others in the Bush administration focused primarily on Israel's interests.

Condoleezza Rice, Bush's national security adviser, on a morning news program, made the argument that when Arafat rejected a peace offer made by Barak, (at Camp David in the summer of 2000), he rejected the "best deal that any prime minister of Israel can ever be expected to give." What she was saying to the Palestinians was this: 'In the future, don't expect any deal better than what you were offered by Barak.' In making this implication, she was creating a ceiling for any future deal. It was an exceptionally irresponsible policy statement, insensitive to Palestinian rights.

Under Barak's offer, Israel would retain sovereignty over the airspace and water resources of Palestine. All the main Jewish settlements deep in the West Bank would remain, becoming part of Israel, and connected to Israel by long tentacles of occupied territory annexed by Israel. This arrangement would divide the West Bank up, separating Palestine into sections, isolated from each other and surrounded by Israeli security forces. There were so many qualifications and conditions that Palestine would not retain any dignity as a sovereign state.

This was a "final settlement" offer, meant to finalize the boundaries. It would have been impossible for any Palestinian leader to accept Barak's offer because their rights under international law were not respected.

Some have argued that Arafat should have given a counter proposal. However, Barak presented an "all-or-nothing" proposal. Besides, the Palestinian position was well known, and Arafat continued to negotiate afterwards towards a fair settlement.

––––––––––––––––––––––––

In June, 2002, Bush presented his peace plan. It was an if-then proposition: If the leadership of the Palestinians adopt democratic changes and reject terrorism, then America would support the creation of a Palestinian state.

Expressed in this simple proposition, it sounds like a good plan. But the plan focused entirely on the interests of Israel. Some analysts commented that the plan must have made Sharon smile, because he could have easily written it. The Bush plan stated that the boundaries of the Palestinian state would be settled by negotiations between the two parties, but made no commitment on what those boundaries should be.

If Bush had said, 'Look, if you people help us put an end to terrorism, we will do everything we can to get your capital in East Jerusalem, remove most of the Jewish settlements from occupied territory, and get just compensation for the Palestinian refugees' Palestinians would be parading down the streets with pictures of Bush, throwing rose petals. And the terrorist networks would have been deflated overnight.

Instead, what the Palestinians heard from Bush was that he wanted them to make changes in their government, which would take one to three years. If this happens, then America would recognize Palestine as a "provisional" state. That means a state, whose powers and boundaries have not yet been agreed upon. Then after that, they get to negotiate with Sharon about the boundaries of the state.

But the Palestinians know that Sharon will not give an inch. They know that his policy is to keep East Jerusalem and the settlements, and maintain as much control as he can over Palestine. And they remember that under Oslo, in 1993, they were also supposed to begin negotiating on the boundaries after two years. Bush's plan did not paint a hopeful picture.

The only leverage the Palestinians have to negotiate is international law and equity. But they need the international community to enforce this law and equity. Without that enforcement, they have no leverage to negotiate. They are at the mercy of the Sharon government.

———————————

Two thirds of Bush's plan was devoted to the democratic changes expected of the Palestinian Authority. The call for reform was welcomed by all. The Palestinians have complained for a long time that Arafat's administration was corrupt. And Arafat, understanding this, called for elections (in January 2003) on the same day as Bush announced his plan.

What was disturbing to the Palestinians was that Bush asked them to remove Arafat. The request was that they should elect leaders not tainted by terrorism. This was not a well thought-out request because most Palestinian leaders have been tainted by terrorism. But more importantly, Palestinians still see Arafat as the "Father" and symbol of the emerging state of Palestine. And democracy, which the Palestinians have been requested to embrace, implies that the Palestinians elect their own leaders, not Bush.

Even Israel's Foreign Minsiter, Shirmon Peres, commented that it was a mistake for Bush to make a Palestinian state dependent on the removal of Arafat. Attempting to salvage things, Secretary Powell has suggested that Arafat be elected to a presidential position with limited powers, giving most of the powers to a prime minister. This would preserve Arafat's status as symbol and "Father" of Palestine.

The Palestinian's idea of reform is a Palestinian Authority that can realize their vision of a Palestinian state. But the Sharon government's idea of reform is a Palestinian Authority that will roll over and accept Sharon's vision of a Palestinian state.

An illustration of this is the arrest of Sari Nusseibeh in the summer of 2002. Nusseibeh is the Palestinian repre-sentative in East Jerusalem, and the Palestinian's most popular moderate. He is an Oxford educated philosopher who advocates the Christian theme of turning the other cheek, and is probably the closest thing to a Palestinian Gandhi. His only crime was political: His presence "compromised" Israel's sovereignty over East Jerusalem. The Sharon government is suppressing even moderates who oppose their policies for a future Palestine.

Like most disputes, the parties to the Middle East conflict are influenced by deep emotions. Israel, a nation of people who have been persecuted for centuries, has an overwhelming need for security. Sharon's policies reveal a man full of fear and anger who needs to strike out against any threat, and to control every inch of the occupied territories. This is exactly the opposite of what is needed to begin reconciliation.

The Palestinians have lived in occupation for decades, and fear that it will never end. It is a feeling like the despair and hopelessness of a drowning man, resulting in violent eruptions. Arafat embodies this. Unable to steer a different path, he has encouraged violence. This is also exactly the opposite of what is needed for reconciliation.

As the mediator, America is meant to infuse rationality into the turmoil of violent emotions. But America is also clouded by emotions: The feelings of friendship with Israel, and the need to appeal to Jewish American constituents. America has failed to be impartial.

The Bush plan is simply not balanced. It represents American intervention for Israel's interests in reforming the Palestinian Authority, but has a hands-off attitude to

Palestinian interests. A mirror image of Bush's plan is the Arab Peace Plan, proposed by Saudi Arabia (in March 2002), and endorsed by former President Jimmy Carter, the father of the Middle East peace process. This peace plan is also an if-then proposition: If Israel withdraws to its 1967 borders, allow the Palestinians to have East Jerusalem as their capital, and reach a "just" solution for the Palestinian refugees, then twenty-two Arab states will establish peaceful relations with Israel.

If we combine the Arab Peace Plan with the Bush Peace Plan, we have the ingredients for a perfect Middle East peace plan. The Arab Peace Plan protects the interests of the Palestinians, and the Bush Peace Plan protects the interests of the Israelis. Protecting the interests of both parties will ensure lasting peace.

After the Bush plan came out, the Arab states of Egypt, Jordan, and Saudi Arabia attempted to combine these two plans by accepting Bush's plan, but adding that after the reforms of the Palestinian Authority, the United Nations should recognize Palestine "based on" the pre-67 borders. Arab states and the Palestinians are thus open to some flexibility in addressing Palestinian interests.

Flexibility in implementing Palestinian interests could result in a fair political settlement, probably along these lines: most of the approximately 150 Jewish settlements in the occupied territory are small and could be dismantled. The remaining few that are essentially towns with thousands of residents could remain, as well as those connected to the borders of Israel. To compensate Palestine for this land, Israel could give Palestine an equal amount of

Israeli land. Some of this land could come from the unpopulated areas of Israel that border Egypt and the Gaza Strip.

Of course, some settlers could choose to stay and live under Palestinian rule. The idea is that the settlers and settlements that remain should not compromise the dignity of Palestine as a state. There cannot be Israeli-only roads connecting Israeli settlements with each other and with Israel, breaking up Palestine. There should be simply Israeli-Palestinian roads. Essentially, settlements should not be used by Israel to divide and oppress Palestine. They should be places that bring Israelis and Palestinians together, economically and culturally. Israel has in the past suggested that they may allow a limited amount of Palestinian refugees to return to Israel. Israel could honor this suggestion and give fair compensation to the other refugees.

Before the recent violence erupted in 2000, the Israeli government was talking of putting parts of East Jerusalem under Palestinian sovereignty. This could be developed. Compensation in land could be negotiated for those Jewish areas of East Jerusalem that Israel may retain. The Temple Mount is already administered by a Muslim trust. It could be put under Palestinian sovereignty with Israeli sovereign rights over the west wall. Or, it could be put under joint administration, or even some sort of international administration.

Finally, Palestine could be de-militarized as was done to the Sinai Peninsula under the Camp David Accords. This would address Israel's ongoing need for security. Palestine would become a Zone of Peace. Palestinians, like

Afghans, have seen too much violence and would welcome a home without guns.

Such a solution would be acceptable by the Palestinian people, fulfill Israel's obligations under international law, and provide the foundations for peace.

_____

The final issue is implementation of the plan. America is forcing Palestinians to make changes. America should also force Israel to make changes. America should come to an understanding with the international community, combining both peace plans into one peace plan. The UN Security Council could pass a resolution sanctifying the peace plan. With America and the full international community behind it, Israel could then be persuaded to implement it. Carter notes that America presently gives ten million dollars a day to Israel, and suggests that America should withhold that money to force Israel to comply with its international obligations.

Another consideration is military aid. Israel has increased its military budget by one and a half billion dollars because of its conflict with the Palestinians. America gives Israel military aid for the expressed purpose of defending itself against aggression. Using its military to enforce occupation is a violation of this understanding. America should withhold this as well.

In actuality, the majority of Israelis support the Arab Peace Plan. It is the small radical Right that want permanent control over the West Bank and East Jerusalem. It is their influence that must be overcome. Forcing Israel's compliance would be a helping hand to the majority of Israelis that are held hostage by a small but powerful minority.

Likewise, virtually all Palestinians support the Bush Peace Plan for democratic changes in the Palestinian Authority. If this is combined with the Arab Peace Plan, then their interests will be protected, and they can no longer be held hostage by a minority of radicals who promote terrorism. These two peace plans, combined into one, would be widely endorsed by both Jews and Palestinians.

To reinforce this foundation for peace, the international community should provide funding for building schools, hospitals, and infrastructure in Palestinian territories. Such an effort is currently being organized under the leadership of Secretary of State Powell. It will help restore the dignity of the Palestinian people and begin a healing process. A half-century of violence, anger, and deep emotional injuries will take time to heal. But at least the foundations for that healing will be set.

Israel and Palestine are small and interdependent. Once peace is established, it is easy to see them becoming united economically, with goods and services flowing freely between the two countries. Perhaps sometime in the future they will cease to see the need for two governments. They will live under one government, and become one people. And their children will read about the decades of war and wonder why.

Part Three: Iraq

Iraq's Stalin

Historians call Mesopotamia, the area of today's Iraq, the "cradle of western civilization." The ancient kingdom of Sumer emerged there six thousand years ago, followed later by the kingdom of Babylonia. The Persians came to rule there, and for a short time, so did Alexander the Great. Arabs came in the sixth century, and Baghdad became the largest city in the world, and the center of Arab culture and world trade. Mongol invaders changed that in the thirteenth century. Then the Turks came on the scene in the fifteenth century, and the area became part of the Ottoman Empire. This ebb and flow of civilization reveals a heritage often forgotten. It also reveals a long history of conflict.

The modern state of Iraq was carved out of the defeated Ottoman Empire by the Allied Powers after World War I. Iraq was administered by the British under a League of Nations mandate, and became independent in 1932 (with continued British influence). Iraq was a land of diverse religious, ethnic, and political groups that resisted British rule. The British responded to this resistance by use of force. In the revolution against the British in 1920, thousands of Iraqi "rebels" were killed, and whole villages destroyed by artillery and fighter-bombers. Wing Commander Arthur Harris, responsible for bombing these villages, was later to become Air Chief Marshal Harris, the architect of "area" bombing of German cities during World War II, such as Hamburg and Dresden.

As a mandate, the British were obligated to establish an Iraqi government capable of independence. They made no attempt to form a broad-based government where the various groups could learn to cooperate. Instead, they allied themselves with just one group, the educated Sunni Muslims, a minority composing about twenty percent of the population. The British used the Sunnis as a power-base, from which they created the Iraqi military and political elite. To head the government, the British imported *Amir* (king) Faisal, a Sunni from Saudi Arabia. Sunni rule consisted of oppressing other groups, mainly the Shia Muslim majority and the ethnic Kurds, and protecting British oil interests. Rule by oppression continued over the decades by a Sunni dominated regime, reaching its nadir under Saddam Hussein.

Saddam came from a Sunni family in the poor district of Tikrit, a community steeped in tribal tradition. In an irony of names, he was born in a village called "al Awja," meaning "the crooked;" and his personal name, "Saddam," is often translated as one who "confronts." With the help of an uncle in the Iraqi army, he received some formal education and exposure to Iraqi politics. He was a bright child, and is said to have a near photographic memory (evidence of the ancient adage that intelligence is not the same as wisdom).

Saddam had an early passion for politics and joined the Ba'ath political party, composed of university students and intellectuals. The party advocated Arab unity. It believed that if Arab states joined together in some form of political union, they would be more capable of resisting the West and Israel. Saddam moved up the party fast, proving to be a talented activist and party enforcer (thug).

Transition between the Iraqi monarchy and the Iraqi republic was violent, with the royal family brutally executed in 1958. General Abdel Kassem, who promised land reform, was made prime minister. The Ba'ath party came to oppose him because he did not support Arab unity. And America's CIA opposed him because he had the backing of Iraq's communist party. Although Kassem was not a communist, the CIA helped the Ba'ath party overthrow him in 1963. Kassem was executed and the Ba'ath party became part of the new government.

Kassem, who had a Shia mother, promoted harmony between Sunnis and Shias. He also helped the poor and recognized Kurdish rights. If America had worked with Kassem to institute land reform, bring the Shias into government, and develop the autonomy the Kurds have always been promised, then Kassem could have led Iraq away from its long history of oppression and violence. There would have been no Iraq-Iran war, no Gulf war, and Iraq would be a great place to live.

It was one of those fateful forks in the road. The CIA chose to help Kassems's enemies kill him, and put the Ba'th party and Saddam Hussein in power. It was this choice that pushed Iraq down into a spiral of oppression and violence.

After the overthrow, the new government began an elimination campaign, killing Kassem supporters, communists, and leftists. Academics, lawyers, writers, students – the cream of Iraqi society – were targeted. The CIA contributed by providing the government with a list of "communists." Hundreds, perhaps thousands were killed, and many more were tortured and intimidated.

In the same year, 1963, the CIA also overthrew the South Vietnamese president, leading to a series of bad presidents. And two years earlier, the CIA organized the failed Bay of Pigs amphibious invasion of Cuba.

The CIA was originally meant to centralize intelligence from various departments. Getting involved in executing policy was a bad idea. It compromised its objectivity as an intelligence gatherer, it did not have the broad scrutiny that the Pentagon and State Department had, and its methods were short-sighted and ineffective. Dean Rusk, who was secretary of state under the Kennedy administration, commented that if the Pentagon was in charge of the Bay of Pigs operation, instead of the CIA, it would not have failed. But most likely, he added, it probably would never have happened because the Pentagon understood the difficulties of amphibious operations, and the State Department understood the political consequences of an American invasion of Cuba. CIA operations have too often resulted in far more evil than good.

When the Ba'ath party seized complete control of the government in 1968, Saddam had risen to Deputy Secretary-General of the party, and had become the head of security. He was the chief thug in Iraq, responsible for oppressing political dissent, and maintaining party loyalty (meaning loyalty to him). He was literally the party whip. Saddam, a ruthless anti-communist, fashioned himself after Stalin, and accumulated a small library on him. For the world, Stalin is a towering icon of evil, equaled by none except for possibly Hitler. But for Saddam, Stalin was a hero. Here was a man who built an empire by the tools Saddam knew best: violence and intimidation. If Stalin could do it, Saddam could do it.

Saddam, the accomplished Stalanist, was able to consolidate his power in just a couple of years. By 1970, he was the *de-facto* ruler of Iraq. The decade leading to Iraq's war with Iran, in 1980, was Saddam's decade of glory. It was during this time that he most nearly fulfilled his vision of being Iraq's Stalin. Saddam expanded his security system, and it became the core of the administration, with spies and enforcers everywhere. His enemies were the usual suspects: Shias, Kurds, communists, leftists, and anyone else who would dare oppose his regime. Thousands were tortured with elaborate methods, and thousands simply disappeared.

Saddam was a master at destroying his enemies, but he was more complex than a simple thug. He understood the mindset of the common Iraqis, and appealed to them directly over radio and television, creating a (false) image of a religiously devout, fatherly figure. He was highly emotional, and used that to give an emotional appeal to the Iraqi people for their support. He also liked children and was a good storyteller.

Saddam supplemented his oppression with highly successful social and economic reforms. He brought modern technology into the market, developed industries, and improved agriculture with sophisticated irrigation. He elevated the status of women, giving them free access to the workforce, including the military where women could go to the military academy and become pilots. By the end of the decade, over ninety percent of women were going to school.

He built hospitals and schools. He hired more teachers and he put the whole country behind the eradication of illiteracy (winning an award from the UN). He brought electricity to thousands of villages, and then distributed free televisions and refrigerators. Saddam changed Iraq. Iraqis became wealthier, healthier, and more educated. This created a large educated middle-class, more capable of asserting their rights. But Saddam was far too accomplished at putting down political dissent to be threatened by a growing middle-class. For all those who were not interested in challenging Saddam's regime, Iraq was a great place. For those who challenged his rule, it was hell.

Saddam's vision of Arab unity evolved to mean that Iraq should be the center of the Arab world, as it was centuries ago. Saddam's ambition mirrored that of Benito Mussolini, who sought to restore Rome as the center of Europe during World War II. Saddam's vision was to be achieved by wealth and military power. To distinguish Iraq from other Arab countries, he began developing a modern military, supplemented by sophisticated weapons of mass destruction.

Western countries sold him advanced military arms and equipment. America's contribution of technology and chemicals led to his program for chemical weapons, the poor country's atom bomb. There were no "smart" sanctions to prevent his military buildup, and Saddam's arm of oppression began to reach outside of his borders. When Saddam formally became the President of Iraq in 1979, he purged his government of those suspected of being disloyal, then began preparing for war. America, having helped put Saddam's oppressive regime in place, also helped make him into the bully of the Gulf.

GULF WARS

The *shah* of Iran was considered a friend to the west
because he opposed the Soviets, and protected western
oil interests. In 1953, the Iranian Parliament decided to
nationalize the oil industry. When the shah opposed this
decision (on behalf of America and Britain), the Iranian
Parliament removed him from power. The CIA and British
Intelligence engineered a coup that put the shah back into
power, and removed a popular prime minister.

The shah was a reformer. He established land reform,
promoted education, reduced poverty, and gave women the
right to vote. But his regime was repressive. He used secret
police to crush opposition and denied basic civil rights.

Because the shah reduced poverty and improved
education, Iran developed a middle-class that became more
and more capable of demanding their rights. If the shah had
allowed for peaceful political change to take place, then the

pressures would not have built up, leading to violent change. But he did not. And instead of a peaceful revolution, there was a violent revolution. The shah, although a repressive dictator by any standard, was not nearly as good at it as Saddam. The revolution, led by the Ayatollah Khomeini, overthrew the shah's government in 1979.

The anger generated by two and a half decades of repression was directed at America, seen as the power behind the shah. "Revolutionaries" stormed the American Embassy and took American hostages. (They were eventually released in 1981.)

For Khomeini, Saddam was another shah. Saddam was a friend of the west that imported western values. Saddam also continued the Iraq history, originally started by the British, of oppressing Shia Muslims. This infuriated Khomeini, who was both a Shia religious leader and the ruler of a Shia nation.

For Saddam, Khomeini was the enemy of all dictators, of all shahs and Saddams. Khomeini's revolution could be imported to the Sunni Arab states – Iraq, Egypt, Saudi Arabia, and Syria – all headed by dictators. He was the Shia equivalent to the Taliban, but not quite so radical. (When the Taliban came into power in Afghanistan, Iran opposed them as being too radical, and as oppressors of the Shia minority, the Hazara.)

Perhaps the central cause of the conflict between Iraq and Iran was that Saddam saw Khomeini's regime as a challenge to his quest for supremacy in the Gulf region. Or, as some explain it, Saddam saw Iran as a stepping stone to his supremacy in the region.

Saddam invaded Iran in 1980 with three hundred thousand troops, beginning a war that lasted eight years and killed over a million people. The irony is that both Saddam and Khomeini were the bitter fruit of an American policy of supporting oppressive, anti-communist regimes.

In the Gulf War between Iraq and Iran, America had a policy of containing the influence of the Iranian revolution. America was basically on Saddam's side. However, America did not want Saddam to win the war, but preferred a stalemate, preventing him from becoming a dominant power in the Gulf. To ensure that Saddam would not be defeated, America gave Saddam three billion dollars in guaranteed loans (which he defaulted on). This money was used to buy arms from Europe and America. American companies sold him helicopters, electronics, chemicals, and other "dual-use" technologies that can be used for either civilian or military purposes. Saddam clearly intended to use them for military purposes.

America continued to arm Saddam up until he invaded Kuwait. Journalists called this "Iraqgate" or "Saddamgate" because it violated laws that prohibited the selling of arms to Iraq, and because of attempts by American officials to keep the facts hidden. America was not alone in its support of Saddam. European and Arab countries also contributed, adding billions of dollars more in loans to Iraq, which used the money to buy more weapons from the West. Feeding Saddam's war machine prolonged the war. A better policy would have been an aggressive mediation effort.

In the end, neither Iraq nor Iran won. Both lost. Khomeini lost any hope of transporting his revolution. The Shia Muslims in Iraq, making up over half the population, never rose up in revolt. Saddam lost because he was deeply in debt from the billions of dollars in loans he received. To complicate matters, the price of oil had gone down, so he was getting less money from Iraq's oil. But from those billions of dollars in loans, he had built a great war machine. And he still had dreams of being the dominant power of the Arab world. All of this made for a dangerous situation.

Saddam began demanding that his loans from Kuwait and other Arab states be forgiven. After all, he reasoned, Iran was a common enemy. This demand was rejected. Kuwait was producing more oil than was agreed upon by the Arab states under OPEC, bringing the price of oil down for everyone. Saddam demanded that they reduce the amount. This too was rejected. Kuwait was taking oil from an oil field that lay on an undefined border between Kuwait and Iraq, and Saddam demanded compensation. And this too was rejected.

Saddam viewed these rejections as economic warfare. And since the rejections were done in personal meetings between Saddam and Arab leaders, they most likely offended a man with great pride, contributing to his decision for a military solution. To add to this, the American ambassador to Iraq told Saddam that America had "no opinion" on the Arab conflicts regarding debts and border issues. There were also American policy statements clarifying that America had no treaty obligation with Kuwait to protect it against an invasion. Saddam invaded, and was surprised when America came to defend Kuwait.

A clear statement from America, saying that an attack on Kuwait would be an attack on America, might have prevented a war. A similar event happened before the Korean war. American policy statements always excluded South Korea from America's line of defense in the Pacific. The Soviets took this to mean that America would not defend South Korea, so they instigated the North Koreans to invade. It is possible that the Soviets would not have ventured an invasion if America had drawn a clear, sharp line.

Iraq recognized Kuwait as a state in 1963. Before then, Iraq claimed that Kuwait had always been, historically and legally, a part of Iraq's province of Basrah. Basrah had been a province of the Ottoman Empire. So most Iraqis reasoned that when Basrah became a part of Iraq, Kuwait also became a part of Iraq. Despite the fact that Iraq recognized Kuwait, most Iraqis still saw Kuwait as part of Iraq.

Saddam took up this line of reasoning for invading Kuwait in 1990. The problem with this reasoning was that it had no basis in modern international law. The modern state of Iraq has never exercised sovereignty over Kuwait. Kuwait came into existence before Iraq. It emerged as a small feudal kingdom in the 1700's under the Ottoman Empire, and paid tribute to the *sultan* of Turkey. From 1899 till 1961 (when it became independent) Kuwait was a "protectorate" of Britain. In any case, modern international law cuts through the tangles of history. When the modern states of Iraq and Kuwait were formed and became members of the United Nations, the ancient feudal relationships ceased to exist.

When Iraq invaded Kuwait in 1990, the United Nations Security Council passed resolution 678, authorizing member states to use "all necessary means" to restore "international peace and security." This was a formality. The United Nations Charter recognizes the "inherent right of individual and collective self-defense." There was no need for UN approval, or for a treaty between America and Kuwait. States had the inherent right to help Kuwait defend itself against an aggressor. The resolution acknowledged this right, demonstrated global support for the action, and provided the involvement of the institutions of the United Nations.

Senator Bob Dole stated that the war was all about oil. Secretary of State James Baker, attempting to get popular support for the war, said the war boiled down to American jobs (I suppose due to the influence of oil shortage). Neither of these reasons resonated with the American people. They were just was not inspiring enough for war. President George Bush, having a better understanding of the American psyche, proclaimed that Saddam was responsible for massive atrocities against his own people, and was committing even more atrocities against the Kuwaitis. He portrayed Saddam as a tyrant who must be stopped. This concept – not cold economic theory – is what resonated with Americans and got their support. Americans like wars that have strong moral foundations.

It is often said that without the oil interest, America would not have involved itself in the war. However, there were other interests. There was the humanitarian interest, just mentioned, that got popular support. And there is the interest in preventing states from annexing other states. Modern international law does not recognize a right of conquest. This is what President Bush meant when he said that the war against Iraq represented a "new world order." There was nothing new about it, except that the end of the Cold War made it easier for the international community to act against aggression.

It is not easy to isolate which interests were the most dominant in influencing America's decision to protect Kuwait. As is often the case, it was probably a mixture of many interests, with particular policy-makers advocating one interest or the other. But the interest of the American people was clear: It was the resistance against tyranny and oppression, the "just cause" of previous World Wars. But what most Americans did not realize at the time was that America helped create Saddam, arm him, and then lured him into war.

BETRAYAL

The Kurds, as a distinct people, have been traced back as far as 2400 BC, where they lived as nomads in present day northern Iraq and Syria. As such, some consider them to be the oldest living culture in Europe. The Greek, Xenophon, complained about their hostility when he led ten thousand soldiers through "Karduchian" villages in 400 BC. Historically, the Kurds tended to organize themselves into a loose collection of tribes, and guarded their independence with great zeal. When the Kurds lived under the ancient Persian Empire, and later under the Ottoman Empire, they refused to be taxed or to be drafted into military service.

After World War I, President Woodrow Wilson championed the principle of "self-determination of peoples" as a guiding light for achieving lasting peace. For Wilson, self-determination was rooted in democracy. It meant the right of "a people" to live free from foreign domination, and the right to choose their own government.

Applying this principle, Wilson decided that the Kurds should have their own state. This idea was incorporated into the Treaty of Servres (1920) between the Allied Powers and the vanquished Turkish (Ottoman) Empire. Under this treaty, Kurdistan would be under a League of Nations mandate system until it was able to govern itself. Kurdistan was to consist of the Kurdish areas in today's northern Iraq, Turkey, and Syria.

However, a new government emerged in Turkey that rejected the Treaty of Sevres. The Treaty of Lausanne (1923) was then negotiated, allowing Turkey, Iraq, and Syria to incorporate the Kurdish areas into their states. The British preferred this new treaty because of the oil fields in the Kurdish areas of northern Iraq.

To compensate the Kurds for the loss of their state, they were given "minority" rights, where their language and culture would be respected. Britain and the King of Iraq pledged to the Iraqi Kurds that they would have their own government. The Kurds would be autonomous, and could govern their local affairs without interference from the Iraqi government. The treaty provisions guaranteeing minority rights and the pledge for autonomy were never honored.

The Kurds in Iraq, who make up about twenty percent of the Iraqi population, continued their long tradition of asserting their independence. The British were the first to make war on the Kurds in order to rule them, using their air power to drop bombs and gas. Successive Iraqi governments followed this practice. The Kurds fought for their autonomy throughout the twentieth century, getting more promises, but little results. The Kurds in Turkey are still fighting for basic rights, and this is the central issue for Turkey's acceptance into the European Union.

The most widely reported event of Saddam's oppression of the Kurds was his use of chemical weapons. Gas attacks occurred a number of times in 1987 without much international attention. But in 1988, western television crews and journalists were able to record the attack of the village of Halabja, which killed around five thousand men, women, and children. Reports and film coverage shocked the world.

The chemical weapon attacks were part of "Operation Anfal," Saddam's extermination campaign against the Kurds. According to official Iraqi records, it has been estimated that about one hundred and eighty thousand Kurds were killed. In addition, about four thousand villages were destroyed, along with orchards, crops, and livestock. This meticulous recording of killings by the Iraqi military is similar to the Nazi records of their death camps. It should not be forgotten that America, with loans and with the sales of technologies and chemicals, helped Saddam develop these chemical weapons.

———————————

The Shia Muslims, living in south Iraq, make up as much as sixty percent of the population. Like the Kurds, they have also presented problems to Iraq's Sunni Muslim rulers, and have been violently oppressed since the days of

British rule. However, they have been less concerned with independence. Their concern is participation in government and basic rights. And they have often appealed to the Shia nation of Iran for help. In response, Saddam had thousands of religious leaders (clerics) and political leaders tortured, imprisoned, and executed. The clerics were targeted because of their connection to the revolutionary ideas of Khomeini. Saddam also expelled thousands of Shias to Iran whom he suspected of having some family connection, however slight, to the Iranians.

Thus, during the Gulf War, when President Bush asked the Iraqi people to "kick Saddam Hussein out," and General Norman Schwarzkopf appealed to them to "rise up in revolt," the Kurds and Shia Muslims took this seriously, thinking America would support them. Shortly after the Americans and their allies stopped the fighting, the Kurds in the north and the Shia Muslims in the south rose up to kick Saddam out. This was their uprising, their *intafada*, after decades of oppression. They soon controlled more than half the territory of Iraq. However, as they proceeded to fight Saddam's troops, the American led army, the most powerful military force ever assembled in the history of the world, stood by and did nothing.

Saddam's troops massacred the "rebels" by helicopter gunships and artillery. Schwarzkopf claimed that America was obligated by the terms of the cease-fire agreement with Iraq to allow Iraq to use their helicopters. This was an empty excuse. By his own admission, they had assumed that the helicopters would be used for non-military purposes. America could have enforced this interpretation.

The rebels were unorganized and had no air power or armor. They could not win without American support. In the south, their cities and towns became reoccupied by Saddam's troops. One to two hundred thousand Shias died under America's watch. (These events provided the background in the movie, *Three Kings*, with George Clooney.)

In the north, Saddam's troops stormed Kurdish towns, causing two million Kurds to flee, many into mountains where they died of exposure in the wet and cold. About one hundred thousand died from military assaults or exposure.

American policy makers made excuses for not intervening, saying that these people have been fighting for centuries, or that they were not innocent because they had put Saddam in power. But the people throughout the world, seeing the images of slaughter on their TVs, knew better. European leaders, especially Britain's Prime Minister John Major, began calling for intervention, and America finally agreed to help.

Security Council Resolution 688 was passed, declaring that the "repression of the Iraqi civilian population...threatens international peace and security." America and its allies set up a "safe haven" to protect the displaced Kurds. "No fly zones" were established to restrict Iraqi gunships, and Saddam ceased his aggression, not wanting to fight the Americans again. However, he had already put down the rebellion.

Because the Kurds have the protection of American air power, they have developed a *de-facto* autonomous region. But otherwise, Saddam continues in his old brutal ways of repression.

It was argued that America and its allies did not have the United Nations mandate to remove Saddam from power, but only to remove him from Kuwait. However, no mandate was needed. Customary international law allows for a state that is defending itself to change the government of the aggressor so it will not attack again. Thus when Nazi Germany was defeated, the Nazis were removed from power, and a new democratic regime was put in its place. The same should have been done with the Saddam regime.

Saddam was not removed because Saudi Arabia and Turkey both preferred to keep him in power: The Saudis, because Saddam's government was Sunni like them, and they feared a Shia-dominated Iraq. And the Turks, because they feared an independent Kurdistan in northern Iraq, bordering the Kurdish areas in Turkey. America bowed to those wishes.

There was also a consideration of potential American casualties in an attempt to remove Saddam. But as in Afghanistan, America had popular support. With Iraqis doing most of the ground fighting, supported by American air power, logistics, and leadership, Saddam would have been easily overthrown.

Ultimately, Saddam was not removed because America gave higher consideration to *realpolitiks* than to the American ideals of human rights and democracy. The British instituted the old form of rule-by-oppression in the

1920's. The challenge facing America was to put an end to rule-by-oppression, and replace it with rule-by-cooperation. The challenge was to get the Kurds, Sunni, and Shias working together in a "broad-based" government. This was the only safe way to ensure a stable and peaceful Iraq. But America and its allies were not up to the challenge. America failed again.

WAR BY SANCTIONS

Instead of removing Saddam and his regime, America led a United Nations effort to make Saddam behave. Harsh economic sanctions were imposed on the Iraqi people, to be lifted only when all weapons of mass destruction were destroyed (and other demands met).

American troops should have destroyed all the weapons of mass destruction at the end of the war, making it a condition of the cease-fire agreement. This would have been quicker and more thorough, and it would have avoided years of devastating sanctions.

In 1995, the United Nations estimated that five hundred thousand Iraqi children below the age of five had died as a direct result of four years of sanctions. Today, in 2002, that number has doubled. Of course, many others above the age of five have been dying too, mostly the young, weak, and old. The total number of civilian deaths due to the sanctions is probably closer to two million. The Arab people are fully aware of the results of these sanctions, generating a decade of anger against America.

Large scale deaths and human suffering are difficult to comprehend. If we follow the life of one individual who has been tortured and executed, and see the consequences on his children and their children, then we begin to feel the depth of the pain. But when we take that one person, and multiply him by just ten, it gets hard to imagine. Multiplying him by one hundred, one thousand, one hundred thousand, or one million, they become merely figures we struggle with to comprehend, but cannot.

Many of these two million deaths were due to bad water, causing water borne diseases like typhoid, dysentery, and cholera. Iraq's water treatment facilities were destroyed during the war, and have not been repaired because of lack of spare parts, due to the sanctions. The most common water purifier, chlorine, is also banned by the sanctions.

Medicine is not available because of the sanctions. Nor do the Iraqis have adequate medical staff or facilities. Simple things like ambulances are non-existent. Lack of food due to the sanctions cause malnutrition, leading to other health problems and diseases (like pot-belly syndrome) that cannot be treated. Mothers suffering from malnutrition give little milk, starving their infants. Although there has been an "oil for food" program, it has produced so little food and medicine that UN officials have been forced to resign in protest. And American citizens who want to bring medicine to Iraq have been subject to fines and imprisonment.

These sanctions are a violation of the law of war that prohibits the targeting of civilian populations. The sanctions also violate the law of war that prohibits war by starvation. And they violate international human rights law that protects the right to health and life. Many have argued that the sanctions constitute genocide against the Iraqi people.

The law of war (humanitarian law) has evolved over the centuries as custom, and is codified in the Geneva conventions. The prohibition against targeting civilians is the most fundamental and oldest law of war. It is often violated, but is universally recognized.

In Shakespeare's *Henry the Fifth* (put on film by both Laurence Olivier and Kenneth Branagh), French knights skirt the British troops and kill all of the British pages (young boys working for the knights). Devastated by the act, a British soldier proclaims that killing boys "'Tis expressly against the law of arms."

Americans would never knowingly approve of a war that targets civilians, with children as the prime target. Yet this is exactly what has happened in Iraq. Death by sanctions is often much worse than death by a bullet or bomb. It is a slow and painful death. The child is in agony from malnutrition, then falls ill. The mind and body waste away slowly, until the end. General Douglas MacArthur once said the highest duty of the military is to protect the weak against the strong. The sanctions are an assault by the strong against the weakest of all.

The targeting of civilian populations began during the war. The air campaign targeted water treatment plants, irrigation pump stations, and electric plants. These are illegal targets under the law of war because they are deemed indispensable to the survival of civilian populations.

America and its allies also targeted insignificant targets in populated areas: bridges, radio and TV stations, government buildings, railroad stations, and the central bank. And somehow, according to Human Rights Watch, they managed to bomb schools, mosques, hospitals, food processing plants, factories, crowded markets, bus stations, trucks, buses, and cars on roads, restaurants, movie theaters, and a couple of hundred houses. Considering that there were 42,000 air strikes, delivering 172,000 bombs, it is surprising that there was not much more destruction.

One of the big lessons of World War II was that the bombing of German cities had no effect in winning the war. It was the bombing of troops, the enemy air force, and fuel supplies that won the war. Without fuel, a mechanized war machine cannot run, and without an air force and army, the war is finished. This would be truer in the shorter wars of Iraq and Afghanistan. The Pentagon has not learned this simple lesson. (Oddly, the "area" bombing of cities in World War II was a British policy. Americans pushed for limiting the bombing to enemy troops and fuel supplies, but lost out on the debate to the British.)

The Pentagon embraces the law of war. It has detailed guidelines, and plenty of lawyers to interpret these guidelines. Military operations must be necessary (not superfluous), proportional (not excessive), and humane (no unnecessary civilian casualties). Although measures were taken to avoid civilian casualties, they were insufficient. These guidelines were stretched almost to the point of being nonexistent.

The Pentagon insisted on attacking the entire infrastructure of Iraq, destroying the Iraqi people's ability to live
and work. This was neither necessary, proportional, nor
humane. It would have been much easier just to destroy the
opposing military. Instead, thousands of Iraqi civilians were
killed in unnecessary bombing and the infrastructure was
destroyed, setting up conditions for two million more to die.

Every American administration has put the blame
for the sanctions on Saddam. After all, they reasoned, if
Saddam had done what America told him to do, the sanctions would have been lifted. This is like a thug who kills a
hostage, then reasons that it was not his fault – it was the
fault of the person who refused to pay the ransom. The
people of Iraq have been held in ransom by American-led
sanctions, and continue to be killed, while Saddam refuses
to pay. Another analogy is the practice of dictators, like
Saddam, who often torture a person's family to force that
person to do their bidding.

In any case, American officials imposed sanctions
with the full knowledge that doing so would result in the
deaths of the weak and helpless. And with the full knowledge that Saddam is not a cooperative sort of person. At the
least, they share the responsibility for these deaths and
injuries with the Saddam regime.

––––––––––––

Long before Nine-Eleven, British and American
policy makers began stating that the sanctions will stay in
place until Saddam is removed from power. This means that

it is no longer enough for Saddam to destroy his weapons of mass destruction. It also means that they expect the Iraqi people to remove him, or at least to help remove him. But the Iraqi people tried, at America's bidding, and were betrayed. After years of Saddam consolidating his power with an all-pervasive security force, it has become much more difficult for the Iraq people to rebel.

The sanctions have also weakened the middle-class in Iraq. These are the people that are vital for changing a government. Some have gone to live in Europe and America, while those who stayed are much poorer, and less educated. Saddam has grown stronger under the sanctions, and the people have grown weaker.

When Colin Powell became Secretary of State, he advocated "smart" sanctions to avoid the adverse affect on Iraqi citizens. The United Nations has recently begun to implement this policy, with some good results. It is a small turn in the right direction. Much more is needed. It would be better simply to lift all sanctions, except the narrow area of arms, and allow the United Nations and non-governmental agencies to begin rebuilding the health care, educational system, and agriculture. America should find another way to remove Saddam. Sanctions do not work.

The only way for America to remove Saddam is to strengthen Saddam's political opposition, inside and outside of Iraq, and work with them. America must teach the Shia, Sunni, and Kurds to work together. If the opposition becomes strong enough, Saddam could be removed with little or no bloodshed, possibly by an inside coup. This is the ideal to strive for.

As this book is going into print, America is debating whether to go to war against Iraq in order to remove Saddam. If America decides to invade Iraq, it must lay the groundwork by using creative diplomacy to win the hearts and minds of the Iraqi opposition, the Iraqi people, and the Arab states. Of course, an even-handed American policy on Israel and Palestine would do wonders in getting their support. Without that support, it will be a long, bloody, frustrating war. But with that support, the bloodshed will be minimized, and the opposition – possibly including parts of the Iraqi army – could do much of the ground fighting with American support, as was done in Afghanistan. And a war that began in 1991, and continued for over a decade through senseless sanctions and occasional bombings, will finally come to an end.

It is not enough to remove Saddam. America must have a vision of a post-Saddam democracy, and a plan to help implement it. Contrary to what critics say, the Iraqi people are ready and willing to embrace democracy. They have seen too much oppression. The British began a tradition of oppression in Iraq that has lasted almost a century. America contributed to that oppression. America now has the opportunity to break that tradition, and begin a new tradition of cooperation, democracy, and human rights. If America achieves this, it will be the first time in history that Iraq has known peace.

The Kurds deserve the permanent autonomy that they were promised almost one hundred years ago. The Shias deserve to have full representation in their government. And the people of Iraq deserve to have a government that protects human dignity. Just as Massoud once envisioned for Afghanistan, perhaps Iraq – with the help of America and the United Nations – could renounce its military and become a Zone of Peace, beginning a new era in the Gulf region. That would be something.

Part Four:
Highest Destiny

FORMULA FOR PEACE

In his little gem of a book, *Perpetual Peace*, the eighteenth century philosopher Immanuel Kant argued that if all the countries in the world were democracies, there would be peace. History supports this theory: Democracies tend to live in peace with each other. A democracy is a system designed to reconcile differences through elections, legislative debates, compromise, and court systems. So it makes sense that democratic countries will tend to resolve their differences peacefully. They are geared for it. America may bomb Saddam's regime or the Taliban, but never Canada or the United Kingdom.

It has also been reasoned that democracies, being sensitive to the needs of the people, are more inclined to protect human rights. And when human rights are protected, there is peace. This reasoning became the premise of the United Nations Charter and the Universal Declaration of

Human Rights. The implication is that it is the accumulated effect of vast numbers of exploited and victimized individuals that erupts into civil wars within nations, and international wars between nations.

Clearly, peace is more than public order. Repressive regimes can maintain public order, but they can not create peace. The Soviets, the Taliban, the Shah of Iran, Saddam Hussein, and Israel's Sharon have all attempted to create peace by oppression. During pre-civil rights America, there was public order, but because of repressive racist laws there was never peace. It was only through the struggles of the civil rights era that peace began to develop. Peace is the fruit of protecting human rights. It is the fruit of resolving the underlying problems that create conflicts. Outer peace is a reflection of "inner" peace.

Conflict is natural to human life. It is through conflict that people are forced to grow. In the case of the civil rights movement, for example, growth means overcoming prejudice. When a conflict is resolved, the fruit of that resolution is experienced as peace. Although conflict is natural, it is not necessary for conflicts to rise to the level of violence. The role of a mediator, and the democratic process, is to facilitate the resolution of conflicts before they erupt into violence.

The most basic source of conflict in the world is the lack of respect for human rights. Individuals and groups are in constant conflict with governments and large businesses, because their rights are being violated. Human rights constitute a vast body of international law, with the Universal Declaration at its core. It includes the civil and political rights we are familiar with, such as equality before the law, freedom of expression, freedom from arbitrary arrest, and the right to free and fair elections.

Human rights also includes the duty of governments to address the economic, health, and educational needs of their people, to protect the rights of "indigenous" peoples and minorities, and to protect the environment. The universality of human rights implies a spiritual unity of the human race. Traditions and values may vary, but they all orbit around core values present in the depths of the human soul.

Our understanding of democracy is refined through the lens of human rights. "Democracy" does not simply mean governments that are elected, but governments that are also sensitive to the needs of their populace in specific ways. It is human rights standards that measure the worth and legitimacy of governments.

A government like Mexico may be called a "democracy" because it holds elections. But it does not represent what most of us consider to be a democracy because of widespread corruption and abuses of human rights. Mexico is thus an "emerging" democracy. Of course, "emerging" and "developed" are relative terms. American democracy is "developed" relative to Mexican democracy. However, American democracy is still emerging, constantly adapting to new challenges; constantly struggling to reach its highest ideals.

Conventional wisdom thus holds that democracy and human rights form the foundations for peace. More precisely, the foundations of peace are the thinking and spiritual forces, stirring within us, that spur us to develop democracies, and to protect human rights. It is this level of humanity that must be cultured and developed to achieve lasting peace.

AMERICA, DEMOCRACY, AND HUMAN RIGHTS

The Revolutionary War was America's first act in the international arena, and the Declaration of Independence was, in a sense, America's first foreign policy statement. The Declaration of Independence was an argument, presented to the world, justifying America's "right" and "duty" to "throw off" the British colonial government. The premise of the argument was that the British had violated the human rights of Americans "to which the Laws of Nature and Nature's God entitle them." American foreign policy was thus born out of the concept of human rights.

The most central right cited was equality. "American" was first used as a derogatory term by the British to refer to second-rate citizens of the British Empire living in America. Before the Revolutionary War, George

Washington was a colonial military officer, acting under the authority of the British. Colonial officers were a lower class than the British officers, with fewer privileges and less authority. After years of attempting to get a commission into the British Army, he retired in frustration to his farm, convinced that he would never realize his dream as a career officer. Washington's frustration was indicative of the relationship between the British and colonial Americans. American frustration built up, and eventually exploded.

This same chemistry for violent explosion has also occurred with the Shia and Kurds in Iraq, with the Afghans under Soviet and Taliban rule, with the people under the shah of Iran, and with the Palestinians under Israeli occupation.

The Founding Fathers were students of natural law philosophy. For them, human rights were not given by governments. They were recognized by governments as already existing, as being "endowed" by God. The American Bill of Rights, as the Ninth Amendment implies, was considered to be a limited and inadequate list of natural rights. The Constitution, as a whole, was thought to be a practical design for a government that would allow people to pursue these rights as they understood them. The exact nature of these rights was seen as only an approximation by society, ever-changing through deliberation.

When Thomas Jefferson was the American minister to France, he advised the French on the drafting of their Declaration of Rights of Man and the Citizen (1789). The model used for the French declaration was the Virginia constitution, containing the world's first bill of rights. Jefferson, like John Adams and most of the other Founding

Fathers, saw the American Revolution as the beginning of a process that would eventually sweep the world and put an end to feudalism and tyranny. The American Revolution, as an ideal of democracy and human rights, was seen as universal, and could not be contained in America. It was the power of an idea.

These high ideals of the Founding Fathers have been severely tainted by slavery, genocide against American Indians, economic exploitation, and legalized racism. But like a theme in an eternal song, they keep reasserting themselves again and again in America, and in America's foreign policy. And each time the theme reasserts itself, America gains a little more depth of its meaning. It's a process of refinement by repetition.

President George Washington advised America not to get entangled in foreign alliances. It was a policy of neutrality. Washington's reasoning was that America was at its infancy and needed time to develop in order to defend itself in a "just cause" against an enemy. Washington thought that at least twenty years was necessary, a few years more than what elapsed between his policy statement (in 1796) and the War of 1812 against Britain. This cardinal advice guided American Foreign policy for about a century, until World War I. It was around this time that America became a world power. And with world power came world responsibility.

President Woodrow Wilson was instrumental in the formation of the League of Nations, from which the United Nations was later born. Wilson declared, as a matter of American foreign policy, that America must "make the world safe for democracy." He also became the champion for the principle of "self-determination of peoples." The idea was that a "people" should not have to live under the subjugation of another people, as the American Founding Fathers had declared earlier. Self-determination of peoples, in the strict sense, means the right to independence. Thus we have India's independence from Britain, and more recently, the Palestinian's call for independence from Israel.

However, self-determination of peoples does not have to take the form of independence. There are other ways for a people to determine their political destiny. In this respect, self-determination of peoples can also mean "minority" rights, where people have the right, for example, to be educated in their own language. And it can take the form of "autonomy" where a people have the right to govern their own local affairs, as the Dalai Lama asserts for Tibet, or the Scotts for Scotland.

Self-determination can also be expressed through federalism. Federalism is based on the premise that national governments must have limited powers to prevent them from becoming oppressive; and that local governments, like America's provincial state governments, should have power over local issues because they have a better understanding of these issues. Federalism creates a dynamic system of checks and balances between national and local governments. Afghanistan is currently in a heated debate on how to share power between the national government in Kabul and the local governments. Of course, democracy itself is an expression of self-determination, where the interests of a people can be asserted and protected.

After World War I, the main global concern was the fate of the newly defeated Ottoman and Austria-Hungarian Empires. The League of Nations "mandate" system was to give self-determination to these territories in two ways: Create nations, based on ethnic, cultural, and economic ties; and establish minority-rights treaties to protect the rights of groups unable to have their own nation. It has been estimated that as much as fifty percent of ethnic conflicts in these territories may have been resolved by this system. No one really knows. The Kurds certainly saw no peace. It was an imperfect solution, and imperfectly applied. But an ideal was born to the world.

The principle of self-determination of peoples was later used as the foundation for the de-colonization in Africa and Asia after World War II, under the auspices of the new United Nations.

Since around 1993, there has been a steady reduction of new ethnic disputes. The main reason for this is that autonomy and minority rights are becoming increasingly more acceptable as solutions to conflicts. The "devolution" of power from national governments to local governments has been going on for a long time in developed countries through federalism and autonomy arrangements. It is now slowly becoming embraced in developing countries. It has taken a long time for Wilson's ideals to catch on.

The last fifty years has seen two apparently opposite movements in the world: The separation of states through self-determination movements, and the integration of states through treaties and international organizations.

Separation movements occur where there is too much control by national governments over a people (as with the Kurds), or over regions (like Soviet occupied Afghanistan, the former Soviet republics, or the occupied territories of Palestine). Integration occurs where there is not enough government, and where there is a need for cooperation and the harmonizing of differences. Thus the United Nations, the World Trade Organization, the European Union, America's NAFTA, Asia's ASEAN, and the endless number of international agreements that integrate the world.

These two movements are the result of one underlying movement seeking a "vertical" balance of powers between the many layers of world organization. At the apex are international organizations, followed by regions, nations, provinces, cities, and villages, all struggling to find their proper role in the political hierarchy. At the very bottom are six billion people demanding their individual right to determine their own destinies. The world is slowly and painfully marching towards global federalism through Wilson's abstract ideal of self-determination of peoples.

President Franklin Roosevelt, in his fight against fascism, declared that the United States must work to establish a "moral order" in the world by promoting the "four freedoms": freedom of speech, freedom of religion, freedom from want, and freedom from fear. "Freedom," he said, meant the "supremacy of human rights everywhere." It was a grand vision to change the world. Eleanor Roosevelt, the wife and "conscience" of Franklin, was the chairperson of the United Nations drafting committee that drafted the Universal Declaration of Human Rights.

At the end of World War II, America lifted the vanquished Germany back on its feet through the Marshall Plan and democratic reform. The same help was extended to Japan. The Japanese people, expecting American demons, met smiling soldiers offering chocolate bars instead. General Douglas MacArthur became American's proconsul (military governor) over Japan, as well as Japan's foreign *shogun*. During his administration he broke up monopolies, established land reform, and presided over the drafting of a new Japanese constitution, unamended to this day, that defined a democratic system and gave women the right to vote for the first time.

This policy of compassion was uncommon in world history, where victors often acted with vengeance and oppression toward the vanquished. Compassion and the encouragement of democratic reform prevented the seeds of tyranny from being planted and thus sprouting in future generations.

Oppressive measures against Germany after World War I fueled the fires of anger and revenge among the German people. Adolf Hitler marshaled these destructive forces, creating a base for his rise to power and his policies of conquest. The Ayatollah Khomeini marshaled the destructive forces created by the repressive policies of the

Shah of Iran, and then turned them against the Shah in a bloody revolution. And bin Laden marshaled the destructive forces created by repressive policies in Soviet-occupied Afghanistan, Arab countries, and Israel, and then turned them against America and other countries in violent acts of militancy and terrorism.

The Cold War was an extension of World War II, and has often been called the Third World War. It is called "cold" only because America and the Soviets never fought directly. But they fought indirectly, and the battles were just as hot and bloody as those in World War II.

The Soviets supported troops fighting Americans in the Korean and Vietnam wars, and America supported the Afghan resistance in their fight against the Soviets. The Soviets took advantage of discontented people living under repressive governments, providing them with the arms and Marxist ideology for revolution. America countered the Soviets by supporting governments resisting Marxist revolutions. This turned much of the third world in Africa, Asia, and Latin America, into a battlefield between two superpowers fighting through proxy armies. The third world became soaked in blood, and littered with injured cultures and dysfunctional governments.

This global conflict often put America in the awkward position of supporting the repressive regimes and dictators that resisted Marxist revolutions. President Jimmy Carter tried to compensate by using human rights practices as a standard for deciding whether to support a regime. Reagan compensated by promoting democracy, declaring that democracy was the greatest defense against communism. It was under the pressure of the Reagan administration that Marcos, Philippine's dictator, and Pinochet, Chile's military dictator, were forced from power. Reagan's policy of promoting democracy resulted in the greatest wave of global democratization ever to have occurred in the history of the world.

The policies promoting human rights and democracy during the Cold War were a healing balm on an otherwise horrific battlefield. They did not prevent the tragedies of the Cold War in Afghanistan, Iraq, Iran, and many other places. But they lessened the pain, and provided a guiding light in the distance. These policies gave America a heart and a soul. And they gave America the moral standing to win the Cold War.

Much of the Cold War was dominated by President Harry Truman's policy of "containment." The Soviets were to be kept in place and prevented from expanding their influence. President Ronald Reagan changed that policy to one of rolling back and defeating the Soviet Union.

Reagan was a visionary, who saw the Cold War as a moral war, with religious dimensions. The Soviet Union was an "evil empire," and America's role was to defeat it. This was opposed to conventional wisdom. All of the foreign policy experts at that time thought it impossible to defeat the Soviet Union. At best, they thought it could be contained in accord with the old policy. Nevertheless, it was Reagan's vision that prevailed.

Reagan defeated the Soviet Union by fighting it on two fronts. The first was military and economic; the second was moral. Reagan forced the Soviets into a costly arms race, countered them in a costly war in Afghanistan (and other areas) and kept sanctions on them. This is the most often cited explanation for the Soviet collapse. However, empires have survived greater hardships. Just look at China during the time of Mao, Iraq under American-led sanctions, or the dirt poor and isolated North Korea.

More important and decisive was the moral front. Reagan appealed directly to the people living under Soviet rule, telling them that their government was evil and was denying them their fundamental rights to freedom and prosperity. This struck a deep chord in their hearts. Many under the Soviet empire, such as Vaclav Havel (who later became president of the Czech Republic) and Andrei Sakharov, were champions of human rights. Reagan helped their cause. Reagan also joined forces with the Pope, supporting the church in Poland in its fight against the communist government.

It was this "moral force," stirring within the people of the Soviet Union and Eastern Europe, that was responsible for defeating the Soviet Empire. It was an internal change. And Reagan used the vast resources of America to inspire and encourage it.

The promotion of democracy and human rights represents the true foundation and the highest ideals of American foreign policy. This is the stuff of *moralpolitiks*, which put morals at center stage, in contrast to *realpolitiks*, which focus only on military and economic forces among competing nations. This aspect of American foreign policy represents America's best and highest destiny.

AMERICA'S LOST VISION

After the Cold War, America's foreign policy floundered. Its role in the world became vague and undefined. America lost its grand vision of changing the world that it had after World War II. America merely reacted to events. American policy became, in a sense, a policy of crisis management.

America punished Iraq severely for invading Kuwait, but did nothing to resolve the problem of Saddam Hussein's repressive regime. When Madeline Albright was asked if American-led economic sanctions against Iraq was worth the lives of thousands of children who died from lack of food and medicine, she responded that it was a difficult decision, but yes, it was worth it. This type of uncreative and unfeeling attitude has dominated much of American foreign policy since the end of the Cold War.

When the Serbs began their aggressions of "ethnic cleansing" in Bosnia, atrocities accumulated over a period of two years before America took decisive action and began a bombing campaign that forced a peace settlement. American policy to avoid the root of the problem in the policies of Belgrade, Serbia, set the stage for the future conflict in Kosovo.

In Somalia, America simply gave up and went home after American soldiers were killed in action. While in Rwanda, America looked the other way as a million people died in a blood bath of ethnic violence. American and United Nations officials knew that this genocide was brewing. There was already a small contingent of UN peacekeeping troops in Rwanda, but when the commander in the field requested five thousand more troops to do the job, he was refused. America could have influenced that decision, but did not. And in Afghanistan and Pakistan, America watched and did nothing as a network of terrorism evolved.

When George W. Bush came into office, his administration articulated a policy of withdrawal from much of the world. America would limit itself to narrowly defined "interests." Israel and the Palestinians would have to resolve their differences on their own. And America would be frugal in providing any troops in peace-keeping operations. American policy was no longer vague. It had crystallized into a do-nothing policy.

American interests were pursued unilaterally. Thus the Kyoto treaty on global warming was declared "dead." No attempt was made to work with the rest of the world, infuriating the Europeans. It would have been a simple matter to address the problems of the treaty by revising it. Here, American policy crystallized into a selfish, America-first policy.

Shortly after President Bush entered office, an American spy plane collided with a Chinese fighter plane (which went down, killing the pilot) off the coast of China, and made an emergency landing on Chinese territory. Bush got on TV and talked in a condescending tone to the Chinese, giving them an ultimatum that if the crew of the American plane were not returned, there would be consequences. At the time, the Chinese had made no clear statement about their intentions regarding the crew. Bush insulted them by portraying them as an enemy instead of a friend. This forced them into a corner. Responding in kind, they called "little" Bush "arrogant and wrong-headed." An otherwise small incident escalated into a crisis.

When South Korea's president visited Washington DC, President Bush remarked that North Korea could not be trusted. This put South Korea's "sunshine policy" of opening up North Korea into a tailspin. North Korea was alienated, breaking down dialogue. Bush's remark was an unnecessary public statement, more suited to private discussions. No American administration ever thought that North Korea could be trusted. That was not really an issue. The issue was how to develop a program with North Korea (to prevent their development of nuclear weapons, and selling of missile technology) that was verifiable and not dependent on trust. Alienating them didn't accomplish this.

The saving grace of the Bush administration was Bush's appointment of Colin Powell as Secretary of State. Powell, although a career military officer, is a consensus builder by nature. Thus, under his counsel, the China crisis was diffused, our European allies were assured that American peacekeepers would fulfill their obligations before withdrawing, and attempts were made to bring North Korea back into a dialogue. But despite this saving grace, the Bush administration managed to alienate much of the world in a few short months, and the American vision of world leadership receded into the mist. Then came Nine-Eleven.

A BOLD NEW POLICY

The September eleventh attack on America "changed the world." It sent a shock wave around the globe, unleashing a fire of horror, fear, anger, and the call for justice. But it also conjured up a deep sense of compassion for all who suffered. The day after the attack, the many peoples of the world came together in silence and prayer for the victims. This was a moment of reflection on our spiritual roots, and it revealed a higher aspect of the changed world.

Those who committed the act, as well as those who supported them, were obviously responsible for Nine-Eleven. But there is another type of responsibility. Those who were capable of preventing Nine-Eleven, but did not, are also responsible. In this respect, America shares in the responsibility for Nine-Eleven. This global tragedy was the result of lazy American policy, primarily on Afghanistan, Israel, and Iraq. Nine-Eleven is the nadir of America's flawed policy of crisis management, of waiting until a problem explodes in its face before it deals with it.

Religious historian Karen Armstrong refers to Nine-Eleven as the "September Apocalypse." "Apocalypse," she points out, means an "unveiling." Nine-Eleven unveiled to America the bitter fruit of its actions in the world. And it thus unveiled its responsibilities to the world.

Suddenly America reached out to the world, and the world reached out to America. American policy-makers were forced to see the need to develop good working relations with the rest of the world. The health of America and the world depended on it. Colin Powell developed such a large "coalition" of nations, he claimed that he had to spend twenty-four hours a day just to maintain contact with them.

Nine-Eleven is forcing America to change its foreign policy. The Bush administration has not articulated a comprehensive policy for America. It has made vague reference to its War on Terrorism as a battle between good and evil, and has branded Iran, Iraq, and North Korea as an "axis of evil." It has also declared American military supremacy in the world, and has embraced the doctrine of preemptive military strikes to counter threats to America. But circumstances are forcing a different, more comprehensive policy.

Whereas Bush advocated a withdrawal from the world, America is being forced to realize it must be engaged in the world. America is being reluctantly dragged into being the global activist. Whereas Bush had stated that America was not into nation building, America is now being forced into nation building in Afghanistan and Palestine. If it is to overcome the "axis of evil," it must also be involved in reforming those regimes as well. America must be the nation builder.

Nine-Eleven has awakened America to the One World concept. America cannot isolate itself behind oceans and fences. It must again find its place in the One World, where every part is interconnected and has a symbiotic relationship to the whole. World interests are now becoming understood to be American interests. This is not a new idea. President Franklin Roosevelt and others have articulated it. But it had been forgotten.

When the Cold War ended, America rested on its laurels of victory. It was a time of indecision. America is now coming to realize that winning the Cold War marked the beginning of a far greater challenge. America's challenge is to help realize the vision of peace on earth. America must be a world builder, helping to build the Global Village.

The maxim, "The best defense is a strong offense," has become popular in describing the strategy of the War on Terrorism. We cannot effectively defend ourselves against every terrorist attack, because it is impossible to anticipate the innumerable ways to terrorize, destroy, and kill. Thus the only effective defense is to engage in an aggressive offense to root out terrorists and terrorist organizations. But if we follow these roots, they do not end with terrorists and terrorist organizations. The roots reach deep into the repressive policies of governments, into poverty, into lack of education, and into human despair.

The United Nations Charter rejects all forms of violence (even the threat of violence) as a political tool. The only exception in international law and Islamic law is self-defense. Terrorism is generally defined as the use of violence against innocent people to spread terror and make a political statement. Both international law and Islamic law reject terrorism as a legitimate form of self-defense. Repressive governments, poverty, or illiteracy cannot justify terrorism. But it has causes. Hate fuels terrorism. Repressive governments and poverty create a breeding ground that cultures terrorism. This is common sense.

Thus, for the War on Terrorism to succeed, it must, like the Cold War, be fought on two fronts. The first front is military and police action. The second front is moral action. This means a massive infusion of American goodwill into the world. This means foreign aid to fight repressive governments by promoting democratic changes and human rights. This means fighting poverty and hunger, and promoting health and education.

Without military and police action, we cannot stop the violence that is in motion. But without moral action, we can never hope to destroy the breeding ground where terrorism and violence are born and cultivated. The War on Terrorism must be fought with compassion as well as with arms.

These two approaches represent America's two powers, the power of peace and war, represented in the Great Seal of the United States. The American bald eagle holds the olive branch of peace in its right talons, and the arrows of war in its left talons. The right is the dominant side, revealing that America's focus is peace, not war.

The prominence of peace is also revealed by the eagle's head, turned to the right: It is facing peace and away from war. The olives on the olive branch symbolize the fruits of peace, the purpose of America.

America's power of war has been used to defeat imperialism in World War I, fascism in World War II, and totalitarianism in the Cold War. It is not now defeating terrorism. America has become the reluctant world sheriff, defending the world against the many faces of tyranny.

America's power of peace is more fundamental. It is the power that gives America meaning and purpose. It gives America a heart and a soul. Peace is a power to be exercised. It is the power of compassion. It is moral power. Peace is not a static state of affairs that comes about by destroying tyranny. It is a dynamic state that must be created by promoting the ideals of democracy and human rights. This is what America is all about. This is its identity.

Terrorism is the tip of a mountain of global problems. Once this tip is dealt with, the human inclination will be to stop its efforts. In times of war, there is a focus of resources, skill, and inspiration that is rarely seen in times of peace. The challenge is to maintain the momentum of resources and energy to eradicate this mountain of problems.

America can maintain that momentum if it comes to realize that repressive governments, poverty, and disease are the root causes of war. Attacking these problems is "preventive defense," comparable to preventive medicine. A world where the main focus is the eradication of poverty and sickness, and the promotion of democracy and human rights, will ultimately be a peaceful and prosperous world.

The Bush administration has come a small way in this direction. It has helped Afghanistan on the path to democracy and has pledged aid. It is pledging a similar aid package for the Palestinians to lift them from poverty. And it has pledged to increase foreign aid from ten to fifteen billion dollars a year by 2006.

However, considering that America produces about one third of the world's wealth (GDP), this contribution is puny. It is not in proportion to its ability or to its heart. Europe, which has less money than America, will be increasing its foreign aid from twenty-five to thirty-two billion dollars a year by 2006, over twice the amount as America.

The Bush administration's main focus is to increase military spending. This is the wrong focus. America is currently responsible for thirty-six percent of all military spending in the world, more than the next eight countries combined. The need for such a large military died with the Cold War. Future conflicts will resemble the war in Afghanistan, where small numbers of American troops are used in coordination with the troops of other countries. What is needed is a small, mobile, highly skilled military working in coordination with other militaries, not a monstrous institution.

The *realpolitiks* military solution to world problems will not work. The military can establish a certain amount of public order, but it cannot create peace. It can defend, but it cannot build a civil society. America can't just beat governments into submission with a stick and expect peace to be the result. And, as CIA operations have proved in Iraq and other places, simply removing a leader from power will not fix things. Governments must be improved from the bottom up. This is the essence of peacemaking.

Nor is the military a complete defense. The rapid development of technology is increasing the potential of individuals and small groups to be destructive forces. Every year, it becomes easier to build weapons of mass destruction, and easier to deliver them. The world's development of technology has surpassed the world's moral development decades ago with the invention of nuclear weapons, and the gap is increasing every year. The only complete defense is to close that gap by building a peaceful world society, which does not breed violence.

What is needed is a *bold new policy* for America. America should base its foreign policy on the premise that the only complete defense to threats is an aggressive promotion of human rights and democracy in the world. In embracing this premise, America would be returning to its ideological roots, to its true nature. It will be making *moralpolitiks* the cornerstone of its foreign policy.

The execution of such a policy would require a change in the priority of resources. Current defense spending is nearing four hundred billion dollars a year, compared to ten billion dollars in foreign aid. This should be reversed. Military spending should be decreased, and foreign aid spending increased.

If we consider foreign aid to be "preventive defense," then two hundred billion dollars for military defense, plus two hundred billion dollars for preventive defense, would result in an unchanged "defense" budget of four hundred billion dollars. At two hundred billion dollars, America's military defense spending will still be larger than Europe's. Considering that peace building is more fundamental than military defense, it is easy to envision a time when the lion's share of money will go to peace building, rather than to military defense.

Global peace building means global democratization. Democracy may take many forms. It does not have to copy the American or British systems. Most people in the world would not want an American electoral system that might result in electing a government that lost the popular vote.

My mentor in constitutional writing, the late Albert Blaustein, use to say that constitutions must be "autochtonous," meaning they must be indigenous, based on the traditions of the nation. The present "transitional" government in Afghanistan was elected by a *Loya Jirga*, a traditional assembly used in the past to elect kings or solve national issues. The Loya Jirga that elected the transitional government was composed of fifteen hundred delegates, and included women and leaders from various professions. They may continue to use it until Afghanistan is capable of having direct elections. And there is no reason why Afghanistan could not incorporate the Loya Jirga as a permanent electoral college.

In addition to free elections, the fundamentals of democracy are a checks and balances system that includes a strong and free media, broad representation in government, and courts and other institutions for mediating disputes. Power sharing arrangements between national and local governments are needed to prevent a concentration of power. And political participation of minorities is needed to protect their interests. Also crucial are independent commissions to prevent government corruption, and to protect human rights and the environment.

These fundamentals are not alien to the world's cultures. They are universal because they are rooted in human nature. Islam, for example, endorses the use of assemblies to resolve conflicts, and mandates that leaders should be loved (not despised) by the people. All cultures understand the need to check corruption and "special interests" through a system of checks and balances. All cultures recognize the need for government accountability, and the need for consensus building and power sharing. Adapting these fundamentals to the traditions and cultures of the world is what makes them indigenous, "autochtonous."

To achieve peace, America must address the world's problems at every level. This is because human rights, democracy, and peace are deeply interrelated. Health, economic development, and education create a middle-class capable of giving a clear, loud voice for reform. Freedom of speech, the "fountain of democracy" allows that voice to be heard, putting pressure on governments. Elected assemblies, courts, and other democratic institutions are needed to give effect to this voice.

Democratization is ultimately a grass roots process. This means energizing the source of democracy, the moral force within people. It is generally understood that reducing poverty will improve education and health, because children can go to school instead of working, and money buys more schools and hospitals. Money also provides the resources citizens need to push for political reform. Improving health will also help to reduce poverty, because healthy people are more productive. And improving education will ultimately reduce poverty, improve health, and create a power-base for political reform.

Educated people know, for example, that people should not drink bad water, and that infants should be breast fed for six months, providing all their nutrients and strengthening their immune system. And educated people are more creative and productive. The economic boom in America in the 1950's and 1960's was largely due to the GI Bill, which paid for the college of thousands of veterans from World War II (including my father). It is often argued that government investment in education results in a profit from economic gain.

Educated people are the primary source of political change. Thus Thomas Jefferson considered free education to be an integral part of a free democratic society. The American Founding Fathers were all students of European and ancient Greek political philosophy, and the American colonists were highly literate. Mahatma Gandhi, who freed

India from the British, was a British-trained lawyer. Nelson Mandela, who led the movement to end South African Apartheid, was also a lawyer. And Andrei Sakharov, who became the Soviet's chief dissident and a powerful advocate for democratic reform, was a physicist.

Reducing poverty, and improving health and education, are thus essential for promoting world democracy. It will create a reservoir of moral force that ascends into the political and cultural arenas of the world, crashing at the gates of repressive and corrupt governments, demanding change.

This is the moral force that created America, and brought down the Soviet Union. It brought democracy to South Korea and Taiwan, and is also bringing the slow cumbersome reforms in China and Iran. It is the underlying current of reform throughout the world, in Asia, Eastern Europe, Africa, and Latin America.

True, a growing middle-class could not reform Saddam. But America is responsible for putting Saddam into power in the 1960's, and killing Iraq's democratic forces of reform. America chose *realpolitiks* over *moralpolitiks*. Now America is being forced to join with the democratic forces of Iraq to get rid of Saddam.

America must also join forces with the people in countries like Egypt and Saudi Arabia, where the governments are resisting the pressure to reform. The goal should not be to overthrow these governments, but to transform them by supporting such things as freedom of press, labor rights and women's rights movements, and institutes of liberal education. Global democratization is a long and frustrating process, and requires the sustained commitment of America and the international community.

Peace cannot be bought. Foreign aid does not mean simply throwing money at foreign governments. It means putting money where it best helps the people of the world. It means intelligent investment.

Perhaps the greatest expression of this grass roots movement in the world is the transnational civil society, working in non-profit organizations such as Save the Children, International Red Cross, Doctors Without Borders, Human Rights Watch, CARE, Greenpeace, Oxfam, and thousands of other smaller, but just as effective organizations.

A global democratization is taking place that transcends governments and national borders. It is, after all, the people's world, and private actors are becoming increasingly involved. America can energize this grass roots global democratization through increased funding of these non-government organizations.

Of course, funds could go into effective UN programs. But they could also go to scholarships for poor students from developing countries to study in American schools, so they can learn about democracy building and take this knowledge back to their countries. And funds could go to establish a new Manhattan Project, composed of the best scientists in the world, to develop clean, cheap (or free) energy, saving the world from pollution, global warming, and the politics of oil. For a creative administration, there are endless ways to promote peace in the world.

When America infuses foreign aid into the world to promote democracy, the result is greater peace and security. But it also results in greater wealth. A healthier and more educated world population creates more wealth. And when nations begin to embrace democracy and the rule of law, they integrate themselves into the world community, becoming wealthier and increasing the general wealth of the world. A wealthier world means a wealthier America. And a wealthier America can afford more money to contribute to the world in the form of foreign aid. This creates an ever-upward spiral of causality.

From the One World perspective, humanity is one multicolored culture, organized into one Global Village. The world's 194 states are neighborhoods in this Village. These neighborhoods are organized through Village meetings and an endless number of Village agreements. Merchants, artists, and visitors travel among them in a steady stream. America composes only about five percent of the population of the Village, but it is the most influential neighborhood. It controls about a third of the Village wealth, and dominates the Village in entertainment (mostly movies), police power, higher education, and technology. But the Village is not a happy place. It is poor, sick, and violent.

Half the people in the world, about three billion, live on less than two dollars a day. Over one billion people live on less than one dollar a day. About one billion suffer from malnutrition. That's a lot of people. If you were to count to one billion, with one count per second, it would take you thirty-two years.

Sixty percent of the people in Afghanistan suffer from malnutrition; in Somalia, it is seventy-five percent. Fifty percent of the people in developing countries suffer from water-related diseases. Forty million people in the world suffer from AIDS, and this is increasing by fifteen thousand people per day.

About sixty conflicts are currently raging in the world. Most of them are civil wars, based on ethnic or religious strife. Of the 192 countries in the world, only 85 are considered "liberal democracies," meaning democracies that attempt to protect basic rights. This represents only thirty-eight percent of the world's population. Of these 85 democracies, perhaps a couple of dozen protect human rights in a substantial way.

Clearly, there is much work to be done. World peace, and the end to world hunger and disease, is thought to be the stuff of dreamers. But the world has the resources and skills to achieve these dreams. What is lacking is resolve and leadership. America can provide this.

Like the Marshal Plan, this *bold new policy* is a win-win proposition. The infusion of large amounts of aid and expertise to promote human rights and democracy will help billions of people around the world. And it will make America safer and wealthier. Instead of anger and frustration echoing back to America from the far shores of the world, it will be love and goodwill. This infusion of compassion into the world represents America's highest destiny. And it will put a new meaning to the term *superpower*.

ABOUT THE AUTHOR

 Roger Plunk was born in England, in an American Air Force hospital. Roger's first love was philosophy, which he studied as an undergraduate. After college he spent time as a sculptor, doing bronze figures. During a trip to India, he was stirred by the poverty and suffering of the developing world. Upon returning to America, he went to law school at Florida State University, and then completed an advanced law degree in international and comparative law at George Washington University.

After a short stay at the U.S. Department of State, Roger went to India by invitation of the Dalai Lama's administration, to advise them in the drafting of a constitution for an autonomous Tibet. He later became involved in mediation attempts between the Chinese and the Tibetans. As an international mediator, Roger also worked on the political conflicts in Burma, Kashmir, and Afghanistan. His first book, *The Wandering Peacemaker*, is about his experiences during this work, interlaced by philosophical reflections. *America's Highest Destiny* is his second book. He has recently formed *Peace Initiatives* (www.peace-initiatives.com) to fund his *pro bono* mediation work.

LaVergne, TN USA
26 October 2010
202402LV00001B/170/A